FEDERAL INCOME TAX LOGIC MAPS

A Collection of Logic Maps Designed to Assist in the Understanding of the Internal Revenue Code

By

Jeffrey A. Maine
Professor of Law
University of Maine School of Law

Series Editor
Sydney A. Beckman
Vice President, Dean and Professor of Law
Duncan School of Law at Lincoln Memorial University

WEST®
A Thomson Reuters business

Mat #41082477

© 2011 Thomson Reuters

    610 Opperman Drive

    St. Paul, MN 55123

    1–800–313–9378

Printed in the United States of America

ISBN: 978–0–314–26899–0

TABLE OF CONTENTS

Editor's Note

The idea behind the Logic Maps came from seeing students' frustrations with the traditional methods of learning federal tax law. This full-color book of Logic Maps, which supports any classroom text, is designed to assist in the understanding of key provisions of the Internal Revenue Code ("Code") and how those provisions interact and generally flow. In most cases, the actual language of the Code is utilized. It is recommended that the actual text of the rules be read and consulted when reviewing these Logic Maps.

The graphical format should help facilitate a method to answering some of the most common federal income tax questions that arise (e.g., whether an item is included in gross income, whether an item is deductible or allowed as a credit, the proper timing of income and deductions, the proper characterization of income and deductions, etc.). Many of the Code provisions contain, to varying degrees, multiple issues and analyses that may be self-contained or involve other provisions. In some cases, treasury regulations, common law, and IRS administrative pronouncements impact the tax analysis and are also referenced. These Maps offer a step-by-step method to help analyze the proper tax treatment of major transactions of everyday consequence to taxpayers. The visual format provides a comprehensive overview, allowing students to review the subject quickly prior to exams.

Feedback

Your feedback is both welcome and requested. Please send suggestions, errors, omissions, or other comments to logicmaps@gmail.com.

About the Author

Jeffrey A. Maine joined the University of Maine School of Law in 2003 as a professor specializing in tax law. Professor Maine has more than sixteen years of teaching experience. Prior to joining the teaching academy, he practiced at Holland & Knight in Tampa, Florida.

Professor Maine is the co-author of five books, and is the author or co-author of numerous articles and reviews on the subject of taxation. He frequently lectures nationally at academic conferences and bar association meetings on taxation.

Acknowledgments

Professor Maine owes special thanks to Tara Wheeler for her invaluable work in building these Maps. He is tremendously indebted to her for her creativity, advice, encouragement, and many helpful insights. Professor Maine also wishes to thank his student, Tudor Goldsmith, for her invaluable work as editor and research assistant.

Series Editor

This series of Logic Maps was conceived and is edited by Sydney Beckman. He is the author of the first book in this series on Evidence. Mr. Beckman is the Vice President and Dean of the Lincoln Memorial University Duncan School of Law in Knoxville, Tennessee. He would like to thank Professor Maine for his tremendous efforts in creating this book.

Legend

Red Indicator

Yellow Indicator

Green Indicator

Indicators are designed to provide a graphical reference similar to stop signs. A red may indicate, for example, that a receipt or benefit is not taxable or that an expense is not deductible. A green may indicate, for example, that an item of income is taxable or that an expense item is tax deductible. A yellow indicator, for example, may caution that an item is partially taxable and partially nontaxable or that an item is partially deductible and partially nondeductible. Both green and yellow indicators typically signal that additional steps are necessary. For example, if a Map indicates that an item is included in gross income, other Maps must be consulted to determine the proper timing and character of that income.

Indicators should be read carefully as the result may differ from Map to Map. In some Maps, for example, green may indicate that an item is tax deductible, whereas in other Maps green may indicate that an item is eligible for a tax credit.

⚠ CAUTION

Caution signs point out pitfalls that students commonly make in an effort to assist the reader in avoiding those mistakes.

⚠ WARNING

Warning signs are designed to warn the reader against starting at an incorrect location or on an incorrect Map.

1

NOTICE

Notice captions direct the student's attention to information that may not be readily apparent. They are also used to provide relevant information that may be found in another Code provision or treasury regulation, an administrative pronouncement, or case law.

This "rough road" sign is used when Maps address particularly complex Code provisions with a number of elements. They are added to make the reader slow down to avoid overlooking details that are being conveyed.

Go to Map x.x

This symbol will direct the reader to a different Map. At times, additional logic is required to be able to continue following a particular Map. At other times, the resulting logic simply takes the reader to another Map for final disposition.

Note

Notes provide important textual annotations. They include, for example, tax definitions, formulae, and ancillary tax considerations that should be considered after a conclusion is reached. They are placed either directly on the body of a Map or they appear as "Notes" that follow a Map.

This Page Left Intentionally Blank

Structure of Federal Income Tax
Overview
1.0

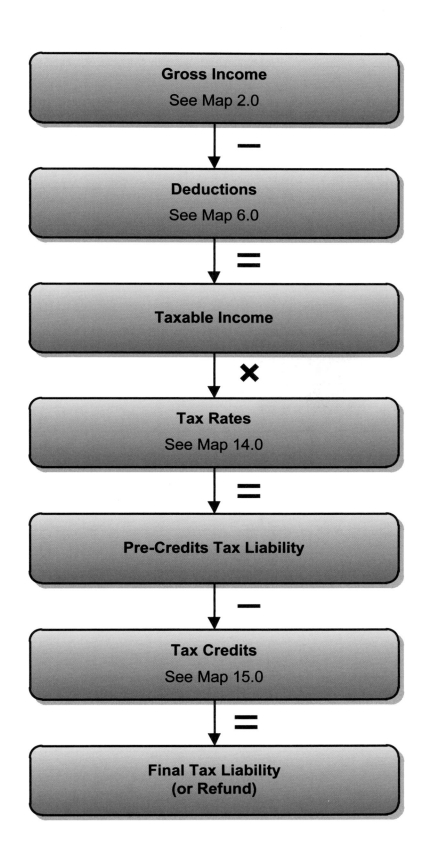

Gross Income

See Map 2.0

—

Deductions

See Map 6.0

=

Taxable Income

✕

Tax Rates

See Map 14.0

=

Pre-Credits Tax Liability

—

Tax Credits

See Map 15.0

=

**Final Tax Liability
(or Refund)**

3

Notes

4

Gross Income
Overview
2.0

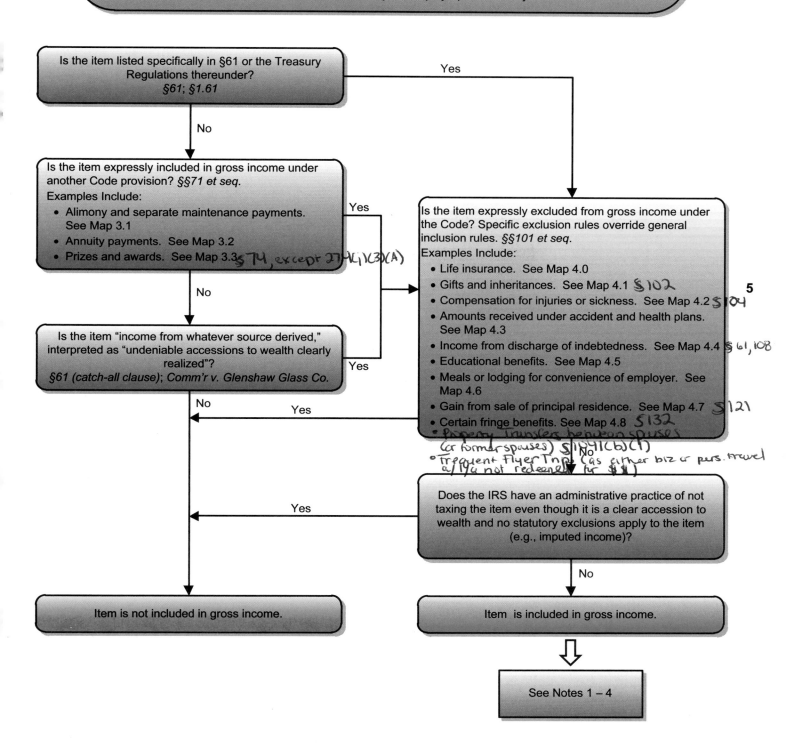

Premise

This Map answers the question as to whether an item is to be included in gross income. Gross income may be realized in any form (whether in money, property, or services), and does not have to be received directly by the taxpayer (e.g., payment of an employee's taxes by his employer). *Old Colony Trust Co. v. Comm'r*

Is the item listed specifically in §61 or the Treasury Regulations thereunder?
§61; §1.61

— Yes →

No ↓

Is the item expressly included in gross income under another Code provision? *§§71 et seq.*

Examples Include:
- Alimony and separate maintenance payments. See Map 3.1
- Annuity payments. See Map 3.2
- Prizes and awards. See Map 3.3 §74, except 274(j)(3)(A)

Yes →

No ↓

Is the item "income from whatever source derived," interpreted as "undeniable accessions to wealth clearly realized"?
§61 (catch-all clause); Comm'r v. Glenshaw Glass Co.

Yes →

No ↓

Is the item expressly excluded from gross income under the Code? Specific exclusion rules override general inclusion rules. *§§101 et seq.*

Examples Include:
- Life insurance. See Map 4.0
- Gifts and inheritances. See Map 4.1 §102   **5**
- Compensation for injuries or sickness. See Map 4.2 §104
- Amounts received under accident and health plans. See Map 4.3
- Income from discharge of indebtedness. See Map 4.4 § 61, 108
- Educational benefits. See Map 4.5
- Meals or lodging for convenience of employer. See Map 4.6
- Gain from sale of principal residence. See Map 4.7 §121
- Certain fringe benefits. See Map 4.8 §132
- Property Transfers between spouses (or former spouses) §1041(b)(1)
- Frequent Flyer Trips (as either biz or pers. travel a/l/a not redeemed for $$)

No ↓

← Yes — Does the IRS have an administrative practice of not taxing the item even though it is a clear accession to wealth and no statutory exclusions apply to the item (e.g., imputed income)?

No ↓

Item is not included in gross income.

Item is included in gross income.

⇩

See Notes 1 – 4

Notes

6

Gross Income Map
Overview
2.0 Notes

Note 1

Proper Amount

What is the proper amount that must be regarded? If property is included in gross income (e.g., treasure trove or property received in exchange for services rendered) the fair market value of the property received is the amount of income reported. If services are included in gross income (e.g., services received in exchange for services rendered), the fair market value of the services received is the amount to be included. *§1.61-2(d)(1)*

Note 2

Proper Timing

When is that amount included in gross income? An item of income must be allocated to the proper taxable year. The proper taxable year is generally governed by the taxpayer's method of accounting (cash versus accrual). See Maps 11.0 – 11.2

Note 3

Proper Taxpayer

Who must report that amount in gross income? Identifying the proper taxpayer is always important. It is governed by the assignment of income doctrine. See Maps 5.0 – 5.1

Note 4

Proper Character

What is the *character* of the item of income? An item of income may be characterized as either "ordinary income" or "capital gain." Ordinary income is taxed at the progressive rates found in §1(a)-(e). Certain capital gains, in contrast, are taxed at much lower rates, pursuant to §1(h). See Map 14.0

Notes

8

Gains (and Losses) from Dealings in Property
3.0

Premise
This Map suggests an approach to examining the tax consequences of property transactions, which can produce either gain (included in gross income) or loss (deductible from gross income). While later Maps address various rules that may impact the tax consequences of property transactions (non-recognition rules, timing rules, characterization rules, etc.), this Map should generally be the starting point.

Is the transaction a realization event – a "sale or other disposition of property"? §1001(a); §1.1001-1(a). See Note 1

No → The transaction is not a taxable event.

Yes

What is the gain or loss *realized* on the transaction?

Gain / **Loss**

Gain Realized = Amount Realized [See Note 2] − Adjusted Basis [See Note 3]

NOTICE
If PS/PG *part sale part gift* see Note 4.

Loss Realized = Adjusted Basis [See Note 3] − Amount Realized [See Note 2]

(not allowed on personal use property §165) only for dispositions of biz or investment properties)

Is the realized gain subject to *nonrecognition* treatment?
- Gain on like kind exchange of property. Map 13.0
- Gain on involuntary conversion of property. Map 13.1
- Gain on disposition of property to spouse or former spouse. Map 13.2
- Gain on corporate formation. Map 13.3
- Gain on partnership formation. Map 13.4

Yes (left)
No

Is the realized loss subject to *nonrecognition* treatment?
- Loss on like kind exchange of property. Map 13.0
- Loss on disposition of property to spouse or former spouse. Map 13.2
- Loss on corporate formation. Map 13.3
- Loss on partnership formation. Map 13.4

Yes (right)

9

No

Is the loss specifically allowed as a deduction under §165 of the Code?
- Loss on disposition of business property. Map 7.3
- Loss on disposition of investment property. Map 7.4
- Loss from personal casualty/theft transaction. Map 8.1

No →

Yes

Is the otherwise deductible loss prohibited or restricted by any other Code provision?
- Loss from transaction between related parties. Map 9.5
- Loss from wash sales. Map 9.6

Yes →

Is the gain specifically *excluded* from gross income under the Code?
- Gain from sale of personal residence. Map 4.7

Yes (left)
No

No

The gain is not included in gross income.

The gain is included in gross income. §1001(c). If installment sale, see Map 11.2.

The loss is deductible.

The loss is not deductible.

⚠ **CAUTION**

See Note 5

Characterization of Gains/Losses
The character of the recognized gain or deductible loss must be determined. In the case of individuals, certain capital gains are taxed at preferential rates. Capital losses are deductible only to the extent of capital gains during a year plus an additional amount.
Maps 12.0 – 12.5

⚠ **CAUTION**

See Note 6

Notes

Gains (and Losses) from Dealings in Property
3.0 Notes

Note 1

Realization events are property transfers that produce a quid pro quo for the taxpayer. Examples include, but are not limited to: (1) a sale of property for cash; (2) a transfer of property to a creditor in satisfaction of a debt; (3) an exchange of property for different property; (4) an involuntary conversion of property in which taxpayer was compensated by insurance or otherwise; and (5) a gift of encumbered property in which the donee assumes the donor's debt. Realization events do not include licenses of property or mere gratuitous transfers of unencumbered property.

Note 2

"Amount realized" from the sale or other disposition of property is the sum of the following amounts:

+ Cash Received (§1001(b))
+ FMV of property received (§1001(b))
+ Recourse debt discharged as a result of the dispositions (§1.1001-2)
+ Nonrecourse debt to which the property is subject (*Crane v. Comm'r/Comm'r v. Tufts*)

Amount Realized

Note 3

"Adjusted basis" for determining gain or loss from the sale or other disposition of property is the <u>taxpayer's original basis</u> (prescribed in §1012 or other applicable provision), adjusted as a result of subsequent events (to the extent provided by §1016 or other applicable section):

11

Step 1: Original Basis

- If the property was purchased → Basis is cost (includes cash paid plus debt incurred). *§1012/Crane*. Note: Some courts disregard nonrecourse debt partly or completely for depreciation purposes if the nonrecourse debt exceeds the property's FMV. *Franklin v. Comm'r/Pleasant Summit Land Corp. v. Comm'r*

- If the <u>property was acquired other than by purchase</u> and included in gross income when received → Basis is FMV at time of reporting. *§1.61-1, -2(d)*. Examples include: compensation of services; t<u>reasure trove</u>; <u>prizes and award</u>; and <u>illegal gains</u>.

  → property is exchanged for other property
- If the property was acquired in a taxable exchange → Basis is FMV of the property received at the time of exchange. *Philadelphia Park Amusement Co. v. U.S.*

- If the property was acquired in a nontaxable exchange or other nonrecognition transaction → Basis is a substituted basis (transferred basis or exchanged basis), subject to adjustments in certain cases. *§§1031(d), 1033(b), 1041(b)(2)*

- If the property was acquired from a decedent → Basis is <u>FMV at the date of decedent's death</u>. *§1014*

- If the property was acquired by gift → Basis is the <u>donor's adjusted basis.</u> Exception: If the value of the property at the time of gift was less than the donor's adjusted basis, then for purposes of determining loss by the donee on a later sale, the donee's basis is not the donor's basis, but instead is the lower FMV of the property. *§1015(a)*   *Either donor's AB or FMV whichever is lower 1015(a)*

Step 2: Adjustments to Basis

- If the property was subsequently improved → Basis is adjusted upward for cost of capital improvements. *§1016(a)(1)*

- If the property was subject to allowance for depreciation or amortization → Basis is adjusted downward for depreciation and amortization deductions taken. *§1016(a)(2)*

Notes

Note 4

Part Sale-Part Gift Situations

Transferor has gain to the extent his AR exceeds his AB in the property. But no loss is realized if AR is less than AB. *§1.1001-1(e)(1).* Transferee has no income, and takes a basis of the greater of Transferor's AB or amount paid. *§1.1015-4.* For allocation of AB in the case of a bargain sale to a charity, see §1011(b).

13

Note 5

If the gain was entitled to *nonrecognition* treatment, the gain is merely postponed until a later year (i.e., when property received in this year's transaction is subsequently disposed of in a transaction in which no non-recognition provision applies). Unrecognized gain is preserved through various substituted basis rules. Maps 13.0 – 13.4. However, if the gain was eligible for *exclusion*, the gain is permanently excluded from gross income.

Note 6

If the loss was subject to *nonrecognition* treatment, the loss is merely postponed until a later year (i.e., when property received in this year's transaction is subsequently disposed of in a transaction in which no nonrecognition provision applies). Unrecognized loss is preserved through various substituted basis rules. Maps 13.0, 13.2 – 13.4.

Notes

14

Alimony and Separate Maintenance Payments
3.1

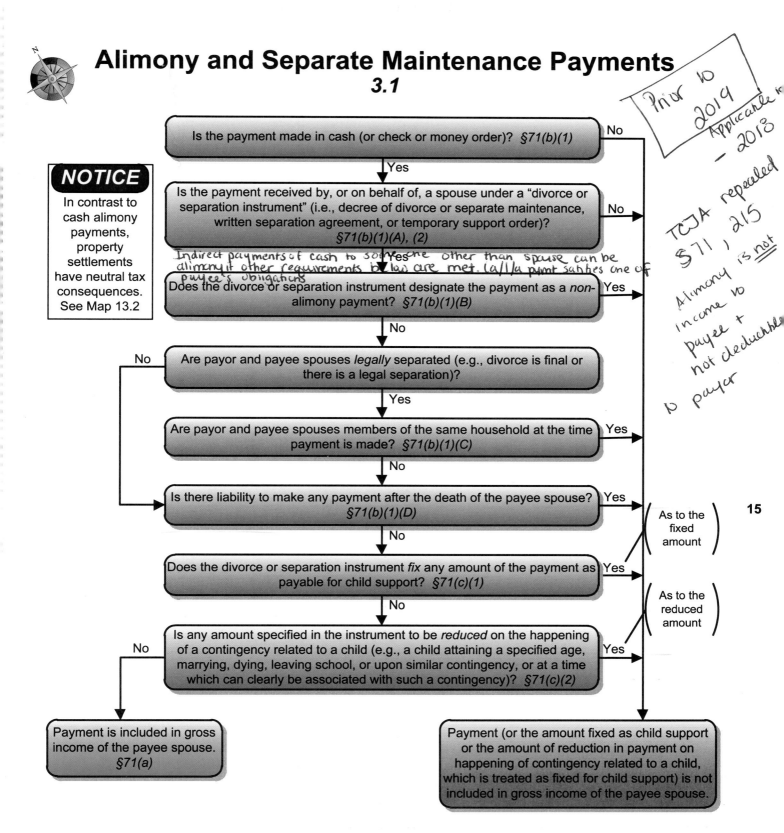

Handwritten notes (top right): Prior to 2019 · Applicable to — 2018 · TCJA repealed §71, 215 · Alimony is <u>not</u> income to payee + not deductible to payer

NOTICE

In contrast to cash alimony payments, property settlements have neutral tax consequences. See Map 13.2

Is the payment made in cash (or check or money order)? §71(b)(1) — **No** →

Yes ↓

Is the payment received by, or on behalf of, a spouse under a "divorce or separation instrument" (i.e., decree of divorce or separate maintenance, written separation agreement, or temporary support order)? §71(b)(1)(A), (2) — **No** →

Yes ↓

Handwritten: Indirect payments of cash to someone other than spouse can be alimony if other requirements below are met. (a//1/a paymt satisfies one of payee's obligations)

Does the divorce or separation instrument designate the payment as a *non-alimony payment*? §71(b)(1)(B) — **Yes** →

No ↓

Are payor and payee spouses *legally* separated (e.g., divorce is final or there is a legal separation)? — **No** →

Yes ↓

Are payor and payee spouses members of the same household at the time payment is made? §71(b)(1)(C) — **Yes** →

No ↓

Is there liability to make any payment after the death of the payee spouse? §71(b)(1)(D) — **Yes** →

No ↓

15

) As to the fixed amount

Does the divorce or separation instrument *fix* any amount of the payment as payable for child support? §71(c)(1) — **Yes** →

No ↓

) As to the reduced amount

Is any amount specified in the instrument to be *reduced* on the happening of a contingency related to a child (e.g., a child attaining a specified age, marrying, dying, leaving school, or upon similar contingency, or at a time which can clearly be associated with such a contingency)? §71(c)(2) — **No** ↓ ... **Yes** →

Payment is included in gross income of the payee spouse. §71(a)

Payment (or the amount fixed as child support or the amount of reduction in payment on happening of contingency related to a child, which is treated as fixed for child support) is not included in gross income of the payee spouse.

Front-Loading of Alimony
(Disguised Property Settlements)

To discourage front-loading of alimony payments (early large cash payments that dwindle in size over a short time), which resemble cash property settlements, Congress added §71(f), which recaptures an amount in the third post-separation year (i.e., the payor has gross income and the payee has a deduction). The recapture occurs in the third year of post-separation payments, but it arises by reference to an analysis of first and second year post-separation payments.

Notes

Annuity Payments
3.2

Premise

This Map addresses §72, which governs taxation of annuities. An annuity is a contract between a contract owner (annuitant) and an obligor (usually an insurance company). Although a variety of annuity arrangements exist, this Map considers the common *single-life annuity*, which calls for fixed future payments to an annuitant for his or her life, received for an up-front payment to the obligor. The amount of each payment to the annuitant is derived by an actuarial calculation that considers the life expectancy of the annuitant and the expected rate of return on the up-front payment.

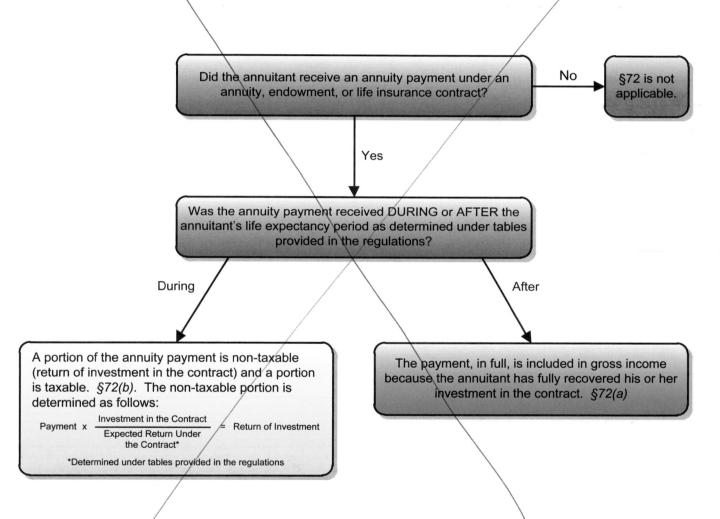

Did the annuitant receive an annuity payment under an annuity, endowment, or life insurance contract?

No → §72 is not applicable.

Yes

Was the annuity payment received DURING or AFTER the annuitant's life expectancy period as determined under tables provided in the regulations?

During

A portion of the annuity payment is non-taxable (return of investment in the contract) and a portion is taxable. *§72(b)*. The non-taxable portion is determined as follows:

$$\text{Payment} \times \frac{\text{Investment in the Contract}}{\text{Expected Return Under the Contract*}} = \text{Return of Investment}$$

*Determined under tables provided in the regulations

After

The payment, in full, is included in gross income because the annuitant has fully recovered his or her investment in the contract. *§72(a)*

Annuitant Who Lives Less than His or Her Life Expectancy

- If an annuitant dies without fully recovering his or her investment in the contract, the amount of the unrecovered investment is deductible on the decedent's final return. *§72(b)(3)-(4)*

- If the annuity contract contains a so-called *refund feature*, and the annuitant dies before recovering the premium paid, the annuitant's estate would receive a refund equal to the excess of the premium paid over the annuity payments received. This refund, generally but not always, is excluded from gross income. *§§72(e), 101(a)*. The value of the potential refund, however, will reduce the "investment in the contract" thereby increasing the taxable portion of each payment during the annuitant's life. *§72(c)(2); §1.72-7(b)*

Notes

18

Prizes and Awards
3.3

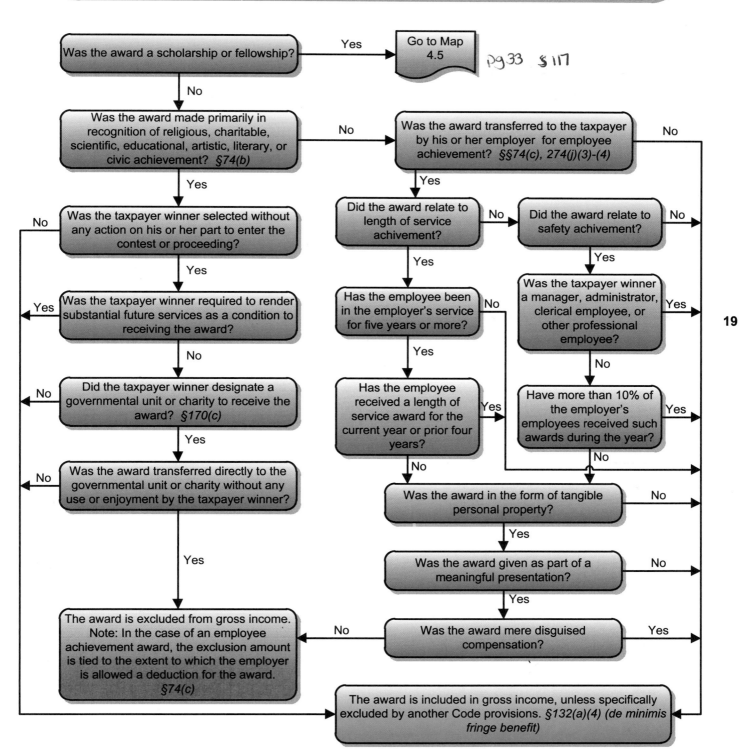

Premise
This Map deals with §74, which expressly includes prizes and awards in gross income but then carves out two limited exceptions.

Was the award a scholarship or fellowship? — Yes → Go to Map 4.5 — Pg.33 §117

No ↓

Was the award made primarily in recognition of religious, charitable, scientific, educational, artistic, literary, or civic achievement? *§74(b)* — No → Was the award transferred to the taxpayer by his or her employer for employee achievement? *§§74(c), 274(j)(3)-(4)* — No →

Yes ↓ (left side)   Yes ↓ (right side)

Was the taxpayer winner selected without any action on his or her part to enter the contest or proceeding? — No →

Did the award relate to length of service achievement? — No → Did the award relate to safety achievement? — No →

Yes ↓

Was the taxpayer winner required to render substantial future services as a condition to receiving the award? — Yes →

Has the employee been in the employer's service for five years or more? — No →

Was the taxpayer winner a manager, administrator, clerical employee, or other professional employee? — Yes →

Yes ↓

19

No ↓

Did the taxpayer winner designate a governmental unit or charity to receive the award? *§170(c)* — No →

Yes ↓

Has the employee received a length of service award for the current year or prior four years? — Yes →

No ↓ (from five years)

Have more than 10% of the employer's employees received such awards during the year? — Yes →

No ↓

Was the award transferred directly to the governmental unit or charity without any use or enjoyment by the taxpayer winner? — No →

No ↓

Was the award in the form of tangible personal property? — No →

Yes ↓

Yes ↓

Was the award given as part of a meaningful presentation? — No →

Yes ↓

The award is excluded from gross income. Note: In the case of an employee achievement award, the exclusion amount is tied to the extent to which the employer is allowed a deduction for the award. *§74(c)* — No ← Was the award mere disguised compensation? — Yes →

The award is included in gross income, unless specifically excluded by another Code provisions. *§132(a)(4) (de minimis fringe benefit)*

Notes

20

Life Insurance Proceeds
4.0

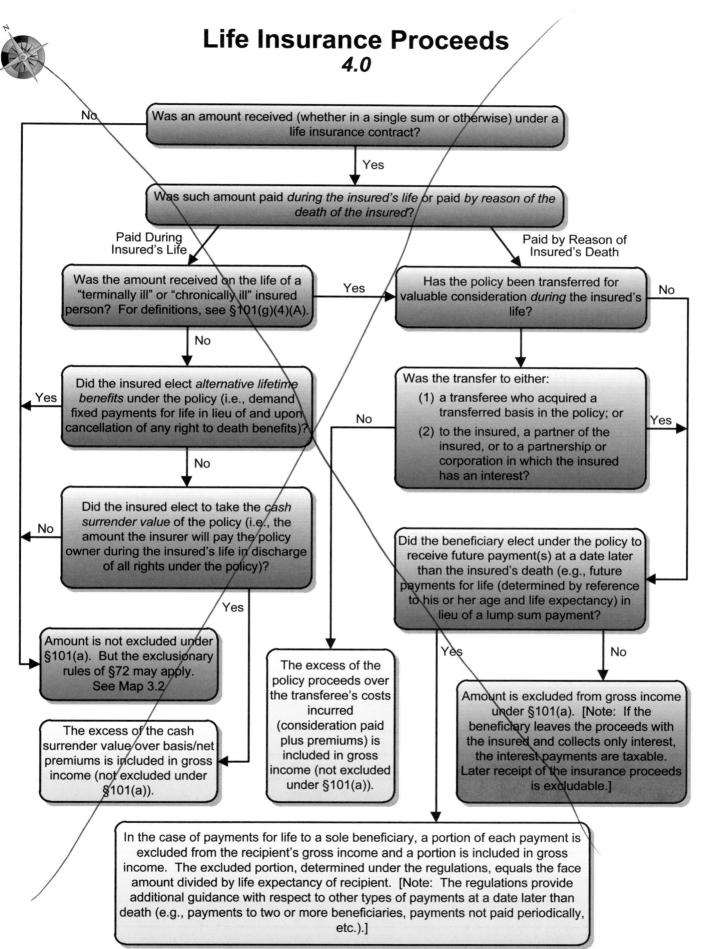

Was an amount received (whether in a single sum or otherwise) under a life insurance contract?

Yes

Was such amount paid *during the insured's life* or paid *by reason of the death of the insured*?

Paid During Insured's Life

Paid by Reason of Insured's Death

Was the amount received on the life of a "terminally ill" or "chronically ill" insured person? For definitions, see §101(g)(4)(A).

Yes

Has the policy been transferred for valuable consideration *during* the insured's life?

No

No

Did the insured elect *alternative lifetime benefits* under the policy (i.e., demand fixed payments for life in lieu of and upon cancellation of any right to death benefits)?

Yes

No

Was the transfer to either:
(1) a transferee who acquired a transferred basis in the policy; or
(2) to the insured, a partner of the insured, or to a partnership or corporation in which the insured has an interest?

No

Yes

Did the insured elect to take the *cash surrender value* of the policy (i.e., the amount the insurer will pay the policy owner during the insured's life in discharge of all rights under the policy)?

No

Did the beneficiary elect under the policy to receive future payment(s) at a date later than the insured's death (e.g., future payments for life (determined by reference to his or her age and life expectancy) in lieu of a lump sum payment?

21

Yes

Amount is not excluded under §101(a). But the exclusionary rules of §72 may apply. See Map 3.2

The excess of the policy proceeds over the transferee's costs incurred (consideration paid plus premiums) is included in gross income (not excluded under §101(a)).

Yes

No

The excess of the cash surrender value over basis/net premiums is included in gross income (not excluded under §101(a)).

Amount is excluded from gross income under §101(a). [Note: If the beneficiary leaves the proceeds with the insured and collects only interest, the interest payments are taxable. Later receipt of the insurance proceeds is excludable.]

In the case of payments for life to a sole beneficiary, a portion of each payment is excluded from the recipient's gross income and a portion is included in gross income. The excluded portion, determined under the regulations, equals the face amount divided by life expectancy of recipient. [Note: The regulations provide additional guidance with respect to other types of payments at a date later than death (e.g., payments to two or more beneficiaries, payments not paid periodically, etc.).]

Notes

Gifts and Inheritances
4.1

Handwritten note (top right):*

To calculate GR see
next page
Gift: AR - Tran. Basis = GR *(Donor's Basis)*
Inherited: AR - Tran. Basis = GR

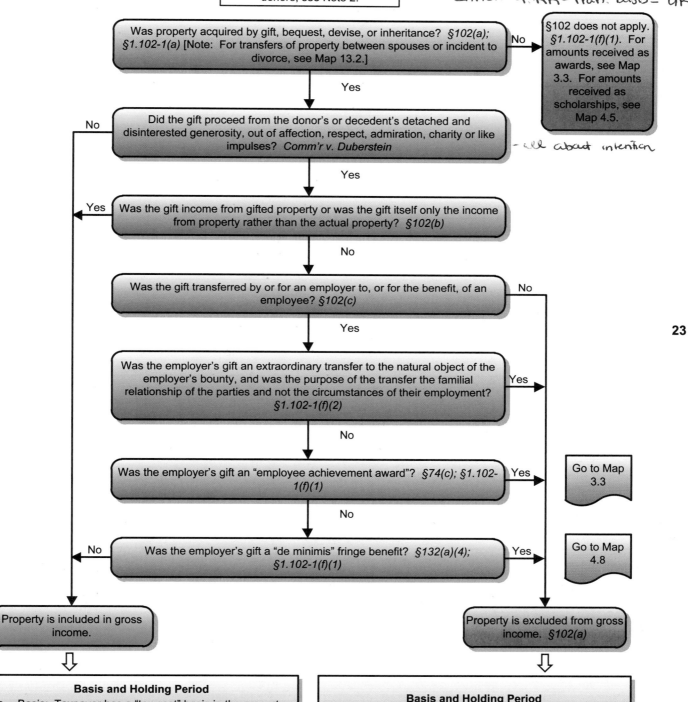

NOTICE
This Map applies to *recipients* of gifts. For tax consequences to *donors*, see Note 2.

Was property acquired by gift, bequest, devise, or inheritance? *§102(a); §1.102-1(a)* [Note: For transfers of property between spouses or incident to divorce, see Map 13.2.]

→ **No** → §102 does not apply. *§1.102-1(f)(1)*. For amounts received as awards, see Map 3.3. For amounts received as scholarships, see Map 4.5.

↓ **Yes**

Did the gift proceed from the donor's or decedent's detached and disinterested generosity, out of affection, respect, admiration, charity or like impulses? *Comm'r v. Duberstein*

(handwritten: – all about intention)

← **No**

↓ **Yes**

Was the gift income from gifted property or was the gift itself only the income from property rather than the actual property? *§102(b)*

← **Yes**

↓ **No**

Was the gift transferred by or for an employer to, or for the benefit, of an employee? *§102(c)*

→ **No**

↓ **Yes**

Was the employer's gift an extraordinary transfer to the natural object of the employer's bounty, and was the purpose of the transfer the familial relationship of the parties and not the circumstances of their employment? *§1.102-1(f)(2)*

→ **Yes**

↓ **No**

Was the employer's gift an "employee achievement award"? *§74(c); §1.102-1(f)(1)*

→ **Yes** → Go to Map 3.3

↓ **No**

Was the employer's gift a "de minimis" fringe benefit? *§132(a)(4); §1.102-1(f)(1)*

→ **Yes** → Go to Map 4.8

← **No**

Property is included in gross income.

Property is excluded from gross income. *§102(a)*

↓

Basis and Holding Period
- Basis: Taxpayer has a "tax cost" basis in the property received equal to its fair market value reported in gross income.
- H/P: Tacking of the donor's holding period does not apply.

Basis and Holding Period
- Basis: See Note 1
- H/P: Tacking of the donor's holding period applies. *§1223(2)*

Notes

Gifts and Inheritances
4.1 Notes

To calculate Basis: and amount to inc. in gross income

Note 1

Basis of Property Received by Gift, Bequest, Devise or Inheritance (§§1014, 1015)

Was property acquired by "*gift*" or "*bequest, devise or inheritance*"?

Gift

Bequest, Devise or Inheritance

Was the value of the gifted property (at the time of gift) less than the donor's basis in the property? — **No**

Yes

Was the (appreciated) property acquired by the decedent by gift during the 1-year period ending on the date of the decedent's death? — **No**

Yes

Did the donee later sell the gifted property at a gain or at a loss?

Did that property pass from the decedent back to the original donor of such property (or donor's spouse)? — **No**

Gain | **Loss**

Yes

Basis is the same basis the donor had (a/k/a "transferred basis").

Basis is the lower fair market value of the property at the time of gift.

Basis is the same basis the decedent had. *§1014(e)*

Basis is fair market value of the property at the date of the decedent's death (a/k/a "stepped-up basis").

NOTICE

If the donor paid gift tax on the gift, the donee is entitled to increase his or her basis (but not above FMV) by the amount of gift tax paid with respect to the gift that arose from appreciation. *§1015(d)*

NOTICE

The basis of a surviving spouse's ½ share of *community property* is stepped up to FMV if at least ½ of the community property is included in decedent's gross estate for estate tax purposes. *§1014(b)(6)*

25

Common law state: surviving spouses entitled to stepped up basis only in decedent spouses ½ of the property §1014(b)(9) + 2040(b)(1)

Note 2

Income Tax Consequences to Donor

- An outright gift of property is not a realization event within the meaning of §1001 because the donor is not receiving anything. Thus, the donor generally has no income tax consequences. However, there are exceptions:

  1. The donor may have gain on a *gift of encumbered property*, with the relief of liability treated as amount realized. See Map 3.0

  2. The donor may have gain on a *part-sale, part-gift of the property*, as the donor is receiving some consideration, and has an amount realized. See Map 3.0

  3. The donor may have gain on the *gift of "section 179 property"* that was previously expensed under §179. *§179(d)(10); §1.179-1(e)*

- A donor may be entitled to deduct business gifts. See Map 7.0

Notes

Compensation for Injuries or Sickness
4.2

Premise

This Map focuses on §104(a)(2), which governs the tax treatment of compensatory and punitive damages received on account of personal injuries and sickness. §104 provides for other exclusions not dealt with here. The tax treatment of business damages is discussed in the note below. For the tax treatment of amounts received under insurance policies, see Map 4.3.

— punishment

⚠ CAUTION

Punitive damages are always taxable. Allocations between compensatory and punitive portions are usually respected if resulting from adversarial, arm's-length negotiations.

NOTICE

Damages received on account of a non-physical injury (e.g., defamation, age discrimination) are not excludable from gross income. However, damages for non-physical injury (medical expenses, lost wages, pain and suffering) that are *on account of* physical injury are excludable. Emotional distress is not treated as a physical injury.

Does the taxpayer receive *compensatory* damages (whether by suit or agreement and whether as lump sums or as periodic payments)? — **No** →

↓ **Yes**

Are the compensatory damages received on account of personal *physical* injuries or *physical* sickness? — **No** →

↓ **Yes**

No ← Are the compensatory damages reimbursing the taxpayer for medical expenses for which deductions where allowed under §213 in a prior taxable year? See Map 8.3 → **Yes**

27

Damages are excluded from gross income. *§104(a)(2)*

Damages are included in gross income (except for amounts paid for medical care attributable to emotional distress).

Business Damages

In determining the proper tax treatment of business damages, the question to be asked is: "In lieu of what were the damages awarded?" *Raytheon Products Corp. v. Comm'r*

- Damages awarded for lost profits are taxable as ordinary income.
- Damages awarded for damage to property, represent a return of capital and are tax free to the extent of basis in the property. The excess may be taxable as capital gains depending on the nature of the property.

Notes

Amounts Received Under Accident and Health Plans
4.3

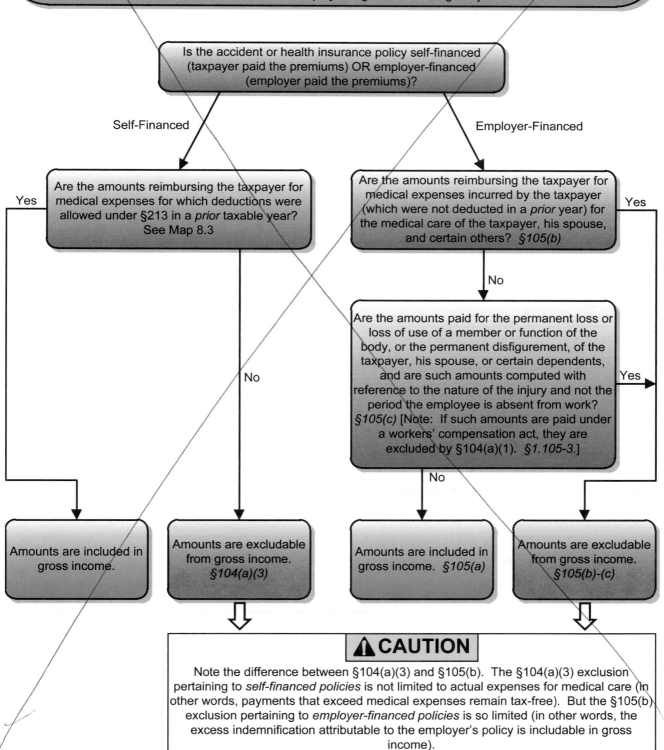

Premise
This Map addresses the tax treatment of "amounts received through accident or health *insurance*" for personal injuries or sickness. The phrase is defined broadly and includes amounts received under an accident or health *plan* for employees. *§105(e).* [An employer's contributions to accident and health insurance plans are generally excludable from the employee's gross income. *§106.*]

Is the accident or health insurance policy self-financed (taxpayer paid the premiums) OR employer-financed (employer paid the premiums)?

Self-Financed

Employer-Financed

Are the amounts reimbursing the taxpayer for medical expenses for which deductions were allowed under §213 in a *prior* taxable year? See Map 8.3

Yes

No

Are the amounts reimbursing the taxpayer for medical expenses incurred by the taxpayer (which were not deducted in a *prior* year) for the medical care of the taxpayer, his spouse, and certain others? *§105(b)*

Yes

No

Are the amounts paid for the permanent loss or loss of use of a member or function of the body, or the permanent disfigurement, of the taxpayer, his spouse, or certain dependents, and are such amounts computed with reference to the nature of the injury and not the period the employee is absent from work? *§105(c)* [Note: If such amounts are paid under a workers' compensation act, they are excluded by §104(a)(1). *§1.105-3.*]

Yes

No

Amounts are included in gross income.

Amounts are excludable from gross income. *§104(a)(3)*

Amounts are included in gross income. *§105(a)*

Amounts are excludable from gross income. *§105(b)-(c)*

⚠ CAUTION

Note the difference between §104(a)(3) and §105(b). The §104(a)(3) exclusion pertaining to *self-financed policies* is not limited to actual expenses for medical care (in other words, payments that exceed medical expenses remain tax-free). But the §105(b) exclusion pertaining to *employer-financed policies* is so limited (in other words, the excess indemnification attributable to the employer's policy is includable in gross income).

29

Notes

Income from Discharge of Indebtedness
4.4

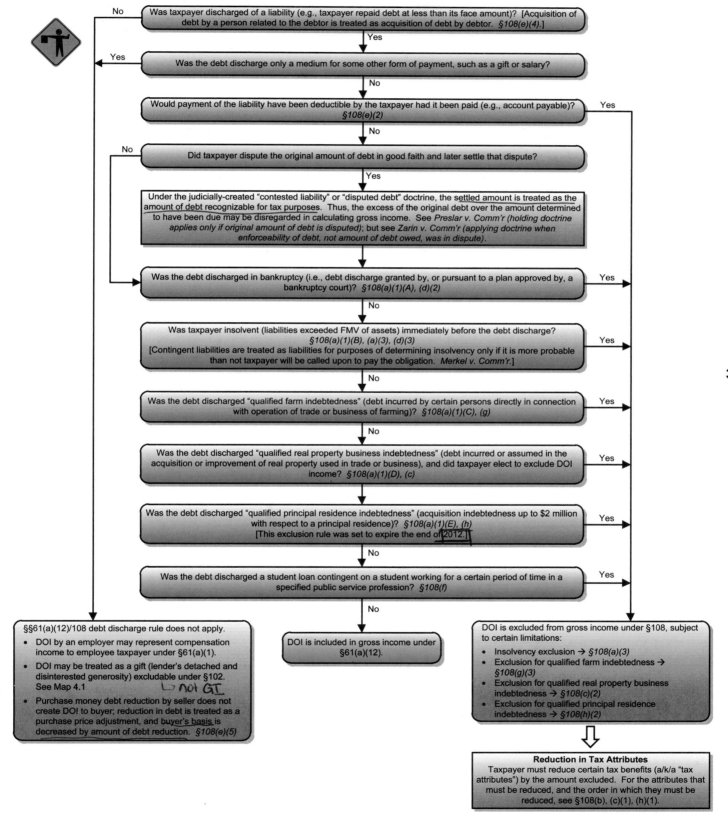

Was taxpayer discharged of a liability (e.g., taxpayer repaid debt at less than its face amount)? [Acquisition of debt by a person related to the debtor is treated as acquisition of debt by debtor. *§108(e)(4)*.] — No →

Yes ↓

Was the debt discharge only a medium for some other form of payment, such as a gift or salary? — Yes ←

No ↓

Would payment of the liability have been deductible by the taxpayer had it been paid (e.g., account payable)? *§108(e)(2)* — Yes →

No ↓

Did taxpayer dispute the original amount of debt in good faith and later settle that dispute? — No →

Yes ↓

Under the judicially-created "contested liability" or "disputed debt" doctrine, the settled amount is treated as the amount of debt recognizable for tax purposes. Thus, the excess of the original debt over the amount determined to have been due may be disregarded in calculating gross income. See *Preslar v. Comm'r (holding doctrine applies only if original amount of debt is disputed)*; but see *Zarin v. Comm'r (applying doctrine when enforceability of debt, not amount of debt owed, was in dispute)*.

Was the debt discharged in bankruptcy (i.e., debt discharge granted by, or pursuant to a plan approved by, a bankruptcy court)? *§108(a)(1)(A), (d)(2)* — Yes →

No ↓

Was taxpayer insolvent (liabilities exceeded FMV of assets) immediately before the debt discharge? *§108(a)(1)(B), (a)(3), (d)(3)* [Contingent liabilities are treated as liabilities for purposes of determining insolvency only if it is more probable than not taxpayer will be called upon to pay the obligation. *Merkel v. Comm'r*.] — Yes →

No ↓

31

Was the debt discharged "qualified farm indebtedness" (debt incurred by certain persons directly in connection with operation of trade or business of farming)? *§108(a)(1)(C), (g)* — Yes →

No ↓

Was the debt discharged "qualified real property business indebtedness" (debt incurred or assumed in the acquisition or improvement of real property used in trade or business), and did taxpayer elect to exclude DOI income? *§108(a)(1)(D), (c)* — Yes →

No ↓

Was the debt discharged "qualified principal residence indebtedness" (acquisition indebtedness up to $2 million with respect to a principal residence)? *§108(a)(1)(E), (h)* [This exclusion rule was set to expire the end of 2012.] — Yes →

No ↓

Was the debt discharged a student loan contingent on a student working for a certain period of time in a specified public service profession? *§108(f)* — Yes →

No ↓

§§61(a)(12)/108 debt discharge rule does not apply.
- DOI by an employer may represent compensation income to employee taxpayer under §61(a)(1).
- DOI may be treated as a gift (lender's detached and disinterested generosity) excludable under §102. See Map 4.1   ↳ not GI
- Purchase money debt reduction by seller does not create DOI to buyer; reduction in debt is treated as a purchase price adjustment, and buyer's basis is decreased by amount of debt reduction. *§108(e)(5)*

DOI is included in gross income under §61(a)(12).

DOI is excluded from gross income under §108, subject to certain limitations:
- Insolvency exclusion → *§108(a)(3)*
- Exclusion for qualified farm indebtedness → *§108(g)(3)*
- Exclusion for qualified real property business indebtedness → *§108(c)(2)*
- Exclusion for qualified principal residence indebtedness → *§108(h)(2)*

⇩

Reduction in Tax Attributes
Taxpayer must reduce certain tax benefits (a/k/a "tax attributes") by the amount excluded. For the attributes that must be reduced, and the order in which they must be reduced, see *§108(b), (c)(1), (h)(1)*.

Notes

Educational Benefits
4.5

Premise
This Map addresses several statutory exclusions for educational benefits, such as scholarships, tuition waivers, and other employer educational assistance. Some of these exclusions apply not only to educational assistance of the taxpayer, but also to benefits to the taxpayer's spouse and dependents. This Map focuses only on the <u>taxpayer as student</u>.

Qualified Scholarship (§117(a))
Did taxpayer receive a scholarship or fellowship grant (amount paid for the benefit of taxpayer to aid him or her in the pursuit of study or research)? — No

Yes

Was taxpayer a degree candidate at an educational organization? — No

Yes

Was the scholarship or fellowship grant used for qualified tuition and related expenses (tuition and fees for required books, supplies, and equipment)? — No / Yes

Qualified Tuition Reduction (§117(d))
Did taxpayer, as an employee of an educational organization, receive a reduction in tuition for education at such organization or another educational organization? — No

Yes

Was the tuition reduction for education below the graduate level, or, if at the graduate level, was the graduate student engaged in teaching or research activities? — No

Yes

Was taxpayer a highly compensated employee of the educational organization? — No / No

Yes

Was the tuition reduction available to other employees so as not to discriminate in favor of highly compensated employees? — No / Yes

Did the scholarship or tuition reduction represent payment for teaching, research, or other services required of the student as a condition for receiving the scholarship or reduction? §117(c)(1) — Yes / No

Educational Assistance Program (§127)
Did taxpayer's employer pay or incur expenses for education of the taxpayer-employee (tuition, books, supplies, etc. or an employer-provided educational course)? — No

Yes

Did the education involve sports, games, or hobbies? — Yes

No

Was the employer-provided educational assistance to the taxpayer-employee furnished pursuant to a program/written plan of employer that meets the requirements of §127(b) (principally does not discriminate in favor of highly compensated employees)? — No

Yes

(As to excess over $5,250)

Did the educational assistance exceed $5,250? [Maximum exclusion is $5,250.] — Yes / No

Working Condition Fringe Benefit (§132(d))
If the taxpayer had paid for the education, would taxpayer have been entitled to deduct the education as a business expense? See Map 7.1 — No / Yes

Benefit is included in gross income.

Benefit is excluded from gross income.

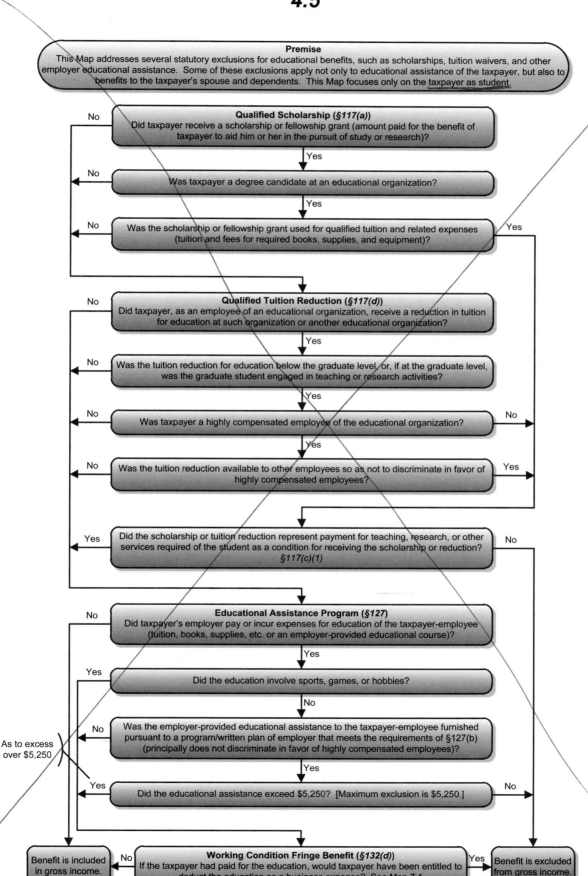

Notes

Meals or Lodging Furnished for the Convenience of the Employer
4.6

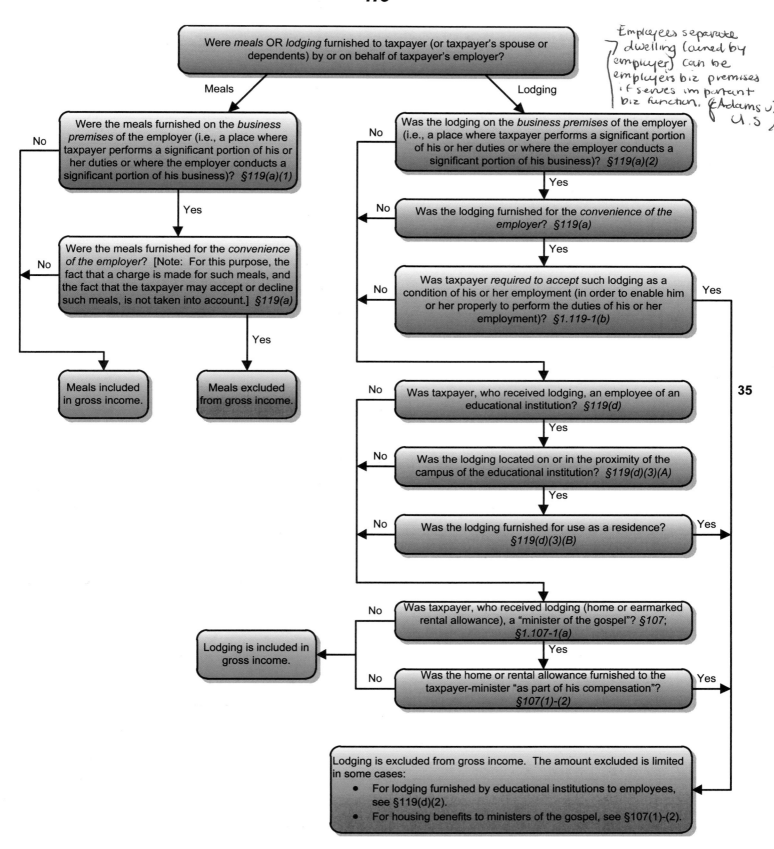

Were *meals* OR *lodging* furnished to taxpayer (or taxpayer's spouse or dependents) by or on behalf of taxpayer's employer?

Employees separate dwelling (owned by employer) can be employers biz premises if serves important biz function. (Adams v. U.S.)

Meals

Were the meals furnished on the *business premises* of the employer (i.e., a place where taxpayer performs a significant portion of his or her duties or where the employer conducts a significant portion of his business)? *§119(a)(1)* — No

Yes

Were the meals furnished for the *convenience of the employer*? [Note: For this purpose, the fact that a charge is made for such meals, and the fact that the taxpayer may accept or decline such meals, is not taken into account.] *§119(a)* — No

Yes

Meals included in gross income.

Meals excluded from gross income.

Lodging

Was the lodging on the *business premises* of the employer (i.e., a place where taxpayer performs a significant portion of his or her duties or where the employer conducts a significant portion of his business)? *§119(a)(2)* — No

Yes

Was the lodging furnished for the *convenience of the employer*? *§119(a)* — No

Yes

Was taxpayer *required to accept* such lodging as a condition of his or her employment (in order to enable him or her properly to perform the duties of his or her employment)? *§1.119-1(b)* — No / Yes

35

Was taxpayer, who received lodging, an employee of an educational institution? *§119(d)* — No

Yes

Was the lodging located on or in the proximity of the campus of the educational institution? *§119(d)(3)(A)* — No

Yes

Was the lodging furnished for use as a residence? *§119(d)(3)(B)* — No / Yes

Was taxpayer, who received lodging (home or earmarked rental allowance), a "minister of the gospel"? *§107; §1.107-1(a)* — No

Yes

Lodging is included in gross income.

Was the home or rental allowance furnished to the taxpayer-minister "as part of his compensation"? *§107(1)-(2)* — No / Yes

Lodging is excluded from gross income. The amount excluded is limited in some cases:
- For lodging furnished by educational institutions to employees, see §119(d)(2).
- For housing benefits to ministers of the gospel, see §107(1)-(2).

36

Gain from Sale of Principal Residence
4.7

If vacation home: Map 9.4

Premise

This Map deals with the §121 exclusion, which is available only with respect to a sale or exchange of a taxpayer's *principal residence*. [Destruction, theft, seizure, and condemnation are treated as sales for purposes of §121. *§121(d)(5)*.] If a taxpayer owns more than one residence, only one can qualify as the taxpayer's principal residence for purposes of §121. The property that taxpayer uses a majority of the time during the year ordinarily will be considered the principal residence. See §1.121-1(b), which provides other relevant factors, including taxpayer's place of employment, the address listed on tax returns, driver's license, automobile registration, and voter's registration, etc.

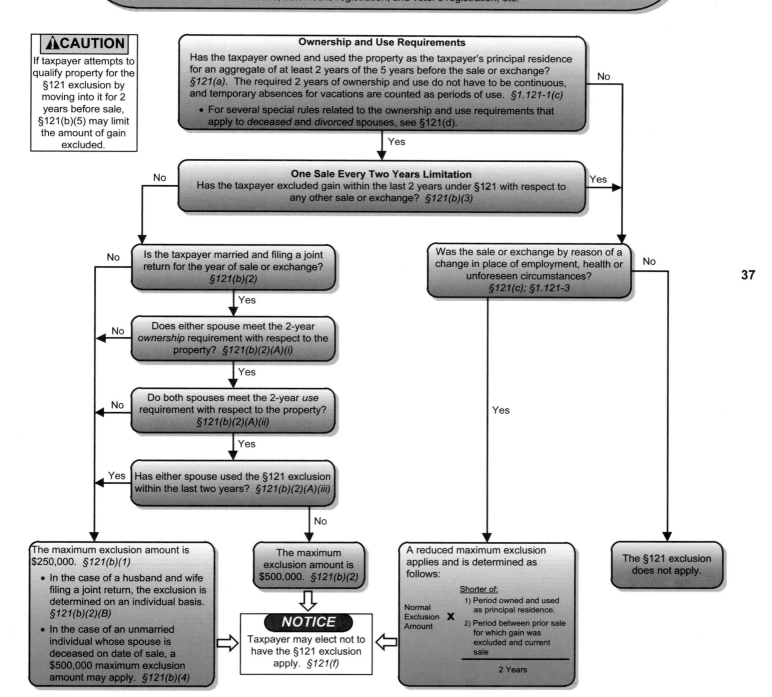

⚠ CAUTION

If taxpayer attempts to qualify property for the §121 exclusion by moving into it for 2 years before sale, §121(b)(5) may limit the amount of gain excluded.

Ownership and Use Requirements

Has the taxpayer owned and used the property as the taxpayer's principal residence for an aggregate of at least 2 years of the 5 years before the sale or exchange? *§121(a)*. The required 2 years of ownership and use do not have to be continuous, and temporary absences for vacations are counted as periods of use. *§1.121-1(c)*

- For several special rules related to the ownership and use requirements that apply to *deceased* and *divorced* spouses, see §121(d).

No →

Yes ↓

One Sale Every Two Years Limitation

Has the taxpayer excluded gain within the last 2 years under §121 with respect to any other sale or exchange? *§121(b)(3)*

No ← / Yes →

Is the taxpayer married and filing a joint return for the year of sale or exchange? *§121(b)(2)*

No ←

Yes ↓

Does either spouse meet the 2-year *ownership* requirement with respect to the property? *§121(b)(2)(A)(i)*

No ←

Yes ↓

Do both spouses meet the 2-year *use* requirement with respect to the property? *§121(b)(2)(A)(ii)*

No ←

Yes ↓

Has either spouse used the §121 exclusion within the last two years? *§121(b)(2)(A)(iii)*

Yes ← / No ↓

Was the sale or exchange by reason of a change in place of employment, health or unforeseen circumstances? *§121(c); §1.121-3*

No →

Yes ↓

The maximum exclusion amount is $250,000. *§121(b)(1)*

- In the case of a husband and wife filing a joint return, the exclusion is determined on an individual basis. *§121(b)(2)(B)*
- In the case of an unmarried individual whose spouse is deceased on date of sale, a $500,000 maximum exclusion amount may apply. *§121(b)(4)*

The maximum exclusion amount is $500,000. *§121(b)(2)*

NOTICE

Taxpayer may elect not to have the §121 exclusion apply. *§121(f)*

A reduced maximum exclusion applies and is determined as follows:

Normal Exclusion Amount **X** Shorter of:
1) Period owned and used as principal residence.
2) Period between prior sale for which gain was excluded and current sale

——————
2 Years

The §121 exclusion does not apply.

Notes

Certain Fringe Benefits
4.8

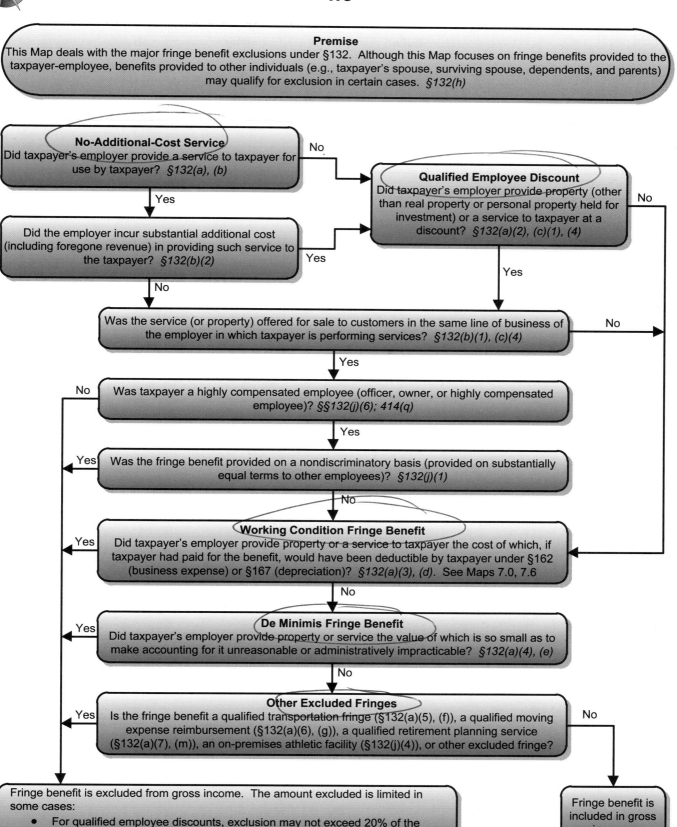

Premise
This Map deals with the major fringe benefit exclusions under §132. Although this Map focuses on fringe benefits provided to the taxpayer-employee, benefits provided to other individuals (e.g., taxpayer's spouse, surviving spouse, dependents, and parents) may qualify for exclusion in certain cases. *§132(h)*

No-Additional-Cost Service
Did taxpayer's employer provide a service to taxpayer for use by taxpayer? *§132(a), (b)*

No →

Yes ↓

Did the employer incur substantial additional cost (including foregone revenue) in providing such service to the taxpayer? *§132(b)(2)*

Yes →

No ↓

Qualified Employee Discount
Did taxpayer's employer provide property (other than real property or personal property held for investment) or a service to taxpayer at a discount? *§132(a)(2), (c)(1), (4)*

No →

Yes ↓

Was the service (or property) offered for sale to customers in the same line of business of the employer in which taxpayer is performing services? *§132(b)(1), (c)(4)*

No →

Yes ↓

Was taxpayer a highly compensated employee (officer, owner, or highly compensated employee)? *§§132(j)(6); 414(q)*

No →

Yes ↓

Was the fringe benefit provided on a nondiscriminatory basis (provided on substantially equal terms to other employees)? *§132(j)(1)*

Yes →

No ↓

Working Condition Fringe Benefit
Did taxpayer's employer provide property or a service to taxpayer the cost of which, if taxpayer had paid for the benefit, would have been deductible by taxpayer under §162 (business expense) or §167 (depreciation)? *§132(a)(3), (d).* See Maps 7.0, 7.6

Yes →

No ↓

De Minimis Fringe Benefit
Did taxpayer's employer provide property or service the value of which is so small as to make accounting for it unreasonable or administratively impracticable? *§132(a)(4), (e)*

Yes →

No ↓

Other Excluded Fringes
Is the fringe benefit a qualified transportation fringe (§132(a)(5), (f)), a qualified moving expense reimbursement (§132(a)(6), (g)), a qualified retirement planning service (§132(a)(7), (m)), an on-premises athletic facility (§132(j)(4)), or other excluded fringe?

Yes →

No →

Fringe benefit is excluded from gross income. The amount excluded is limited in some cases:
- For qualified employee discounts, exclusion may not exceed 20% of the retail price in the case of *services* or the gross profit percentage in the case of *property*. *§132(c)*
- For qualified transportation fringes, see §132(f)(2).

Fringe benefit is included in gross income.

39

Notes

40

Assignments of Earned Income
5.0

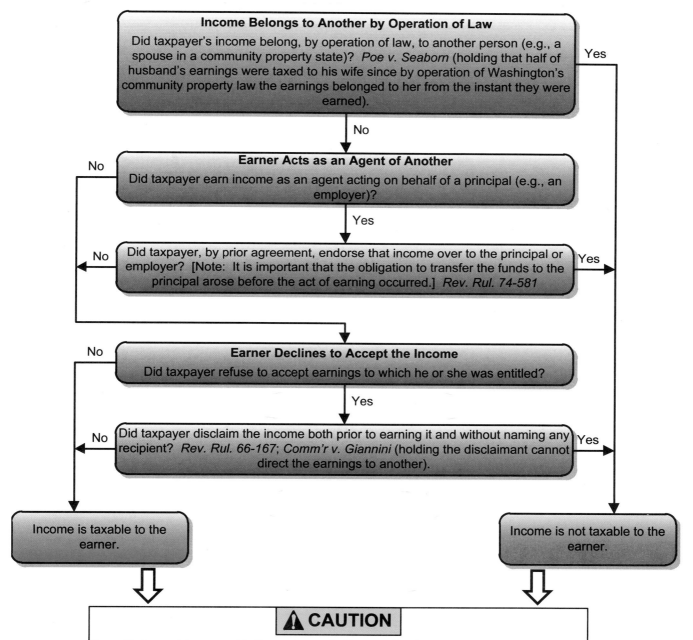

Premise

Under the "assignment of income doctrine," income is taxed to the person who earned it. *Lucas v. Earl*. This Map considers important exceptions to this basic rule. [Note: For rules governing assignments of income from property, see Map 5.1.]

Income Belongs to Another by Operation of Law

Did taxpayer's income belong, by operation of law, to another person (e.g., a spouse in a community property state)? *Poe v. Seaborn* (holding that half of husband's earnings were taxed to his wife since by operation of Washington's community property law the earnings belonged to her from the instant they were earned).

Yes

No

Earner Acts as an Agent of Another

Did taxpayer earn income as an agent acting on behalf of a principal (e.g., an employer)?

No

Yes

Did taxpayer, by prior agreement, endorse that income over to the principal or employer? [Note: It is important that the obligation to transfer the funds to the principal arose before the act of earning occurred.] *Rev. Rul. 74-581*

No

Yes

Earner Declines to Accept the Income

Did taxpayer refuse to accept earnings to which he or she was entitled?

No

Yes

Did taxpayer disclaim the income both prior to earning it and without naming any recipient? *Rev. Rul. 66-167*; *Comm'r v. Giannini* (holding the disclaimant cannot direct the earnings to another).

No

Yes

Income is taxable to the earner.

Income is not taxable to the earner.

⚠ CAUTION

Some Code provisions override the assignment of income doctrine:
- §66 → Each spouse's earned community income is treated as separate for tax purposes in certain hardship cases.
- §73 → A child's earned income is taxed to the child, not the parent, even though state law deems that income property of the parent.
- §351 → When there is a valid business purpose for the transfer of accounts receivable on the incorporation of an ongoing business, the transferee corporation will report the receivables in income as collected. *Hempt Brothers, Inc. v. United States*

Notes

Assignments of Income from Property
5.1

Premise

As a general rule, the owner of property is taxed on the income from the property. This Map considers judicial and statutory restraints on the assignment of income from property. It answers the question who is taxable on income if (1) a property owner transfers the right to receive the income from the property to another while retaining the property itself, or (2) a property owner transfers the property that produces the income. [Note: For rules governing assignments of income from services, see Map 5.0.]

Did taxpayer transfer the right to receive income from property to another person while retaining the property itself OR did taxpayer transfer the actually property that produces the income?

Transfer of Right to Receive Income

Transfer of Property that Produces Income

Was the assignment of income for valuable consideration (i.e., taxpayer sold the right to future income) OR was the assignment of income gratuitous?

Was income already realized or accrued at the time of the assignment of property?

For Valuable Consideration

Gratuitous

Yes

No

If the transaction is a bona fide sale, it is respected for tax purposes and governed by §1001. Taxpayer's amount realized is income as taxpayer has a zero basis in pre-tax income. *Estate of Stranahan v. Comm'r*
Note: The transaction will not be respected as a bona fide sale if it merely produces a loan-type investment secured by the right to future income. *Mapco, Inc. v. United States*

Taxpayer-owner of the property remains taxable on the income. *Helvering v. Horst*

The assignee, and not the taxpayer, is taxable on the income from the property. Income from property can be effectively assigned if taxpayer gives the property away.

43

⚠ **CAUTION**

Statutory Restraints on Assignment of Income from Property

- **Transfers to Trusts**: The grantor trust rules (§§ 671-79) provide that if a grantor sets up a trust but retains any of a number of different rights (e.g., right to revoke), the trust income remains taxable to the grantor. Also, the rate structure applicable to trusts (§1(e)) is less graduated than the rate structure for individuals.

- **Transfers to Children**: Most unearned income of a child under the age of 18 is taxed at the child's parents' top marginal rate. See Map 14.2

[handwritten: or is it taxed @ same rate as T+Es?]

Notes

Deductions
Overview
6.0

Handwritten note (top right):
sp. biz attire
incidental repairs
material + supplies
rent for use of prop.
reasonable salaries

Premise
Deductions are a matter of legislative grace. While there are various Code provisions that prescribe deductions (§§161-198, 211-222), there are some overriding Code provisions that expressly limit or disallow what was otherwise authorized (§§261-280H). This Map illustrates this give and take, and provides an overview of key deduction provisions that are explored in more detail in other Maps.

Handwritten note (left): applies to employees

Handwritten note (right):
- ordinary + necessary 7.0(gen)
- biz education exp. 7.1
- biz travel exp. 7.2
- other - interest, losses + bad debts

Business Deductions
Is the item authorized as a trade or business deduction? See Maps 7.0-7.3 — Yes

No

Investment/Profit-Making Deductions
Although not incurred in a business activity, is the item connected with an income or profit-seeking activity so as to be authorized as a deduction? See Map 7.4 — Yes

No

Personal Deductions
Although not incurred in a business, income, or profit-seeking activity, is the item nevertheless authorized by the Code as a deduction? Examples include: — Yes
- Qualified residence interest. See Map 8.0
- Casualty losses. See Map 8.1
- Charitable gifts. See Map 8.2
- Medical expenses. See Map 8.3
- Alimony. See Map 8.4
- Moving expenses. See Map 8.5
- Personal and dependency exemptions. See Map 10.1

Handwritten note (right):
262 prohibits deductions for "personal, living, or family expenses."

Nondeductible Capital Expenditures — No
Is the business, investment, or personal item (otherwise authorized by the Code) classified as a nondeductible capital expenditure? See Map 7.5

45

Yes

Depreciation and Amortization Deductions — Yes
Is the capital expenditure eligible to be deducted over time through an authorized depreciation or amortization allowance? See Maps 7.6-7.7 — No

Restrictions on Deductions
Does an overriding Code provision expressly *limit* or *deny* what was otherwise authorized? Examples include:
- §183, Hobby Losses. See Map 9.0
- §465, The At Risk Rules. See Map 9.1
- §469, The Passive Loss Rules. See Map 9.2
- §280A, Home Office Deductions. See Map 9.3
- §280A, Vacation Home Deductions. See Map 9.4
- §267, Losses Between Related Parties. See Map 9.5
- §1091, Losses from Wash Sales of Stock. See Map 9.6

No

Yes, deny

Yes, limit

Deduction is fully allowed.

Deduction is limited.

Deduction is not allowed.

Deduction Considerations
After determining whether an item is partially or fully deductible, there are several questions that must be addressed:
- **Proper Timing.** When is the item deducted from gross income? A deduction must be allocated to the proper taxable year. The proper taxable year is generally governed by taxpayer's method of accounting (cash or accrual). See Maps 11.0-11.1
- **Proper Character.** What is the character of the deduction? A deduction may be characterized as either ordinary or capital. Capital losses are subject to a statutory restriction. See Maps 12.0-12.1, 12.5
- **Deduction Hierarchy.** Where in the tax calculation is the deduction taken? Some deductions are taken from gross income in arriving at adjusted gross income. Other deductions are taken from adjusted gross income in arriving at taxable income. See Map 10.0

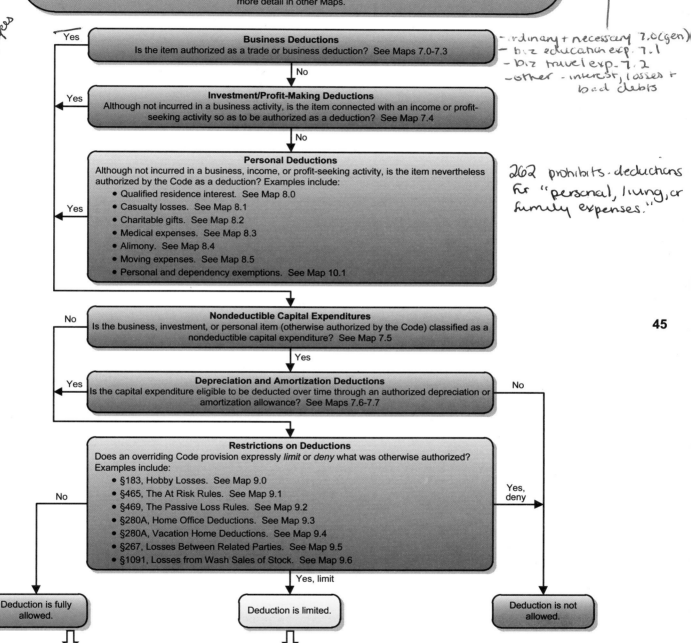

Notes

46

Section 162: Trade or Business Expenses
7.0

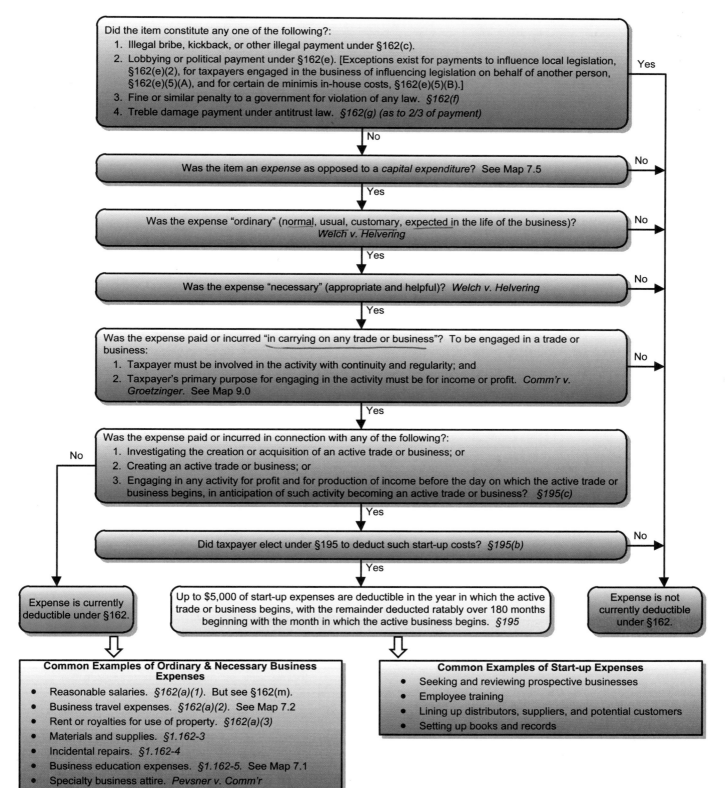

Did the item constitute any one of the following?:
1. Illegal bribe, kickback, or other illegal payment under §162(c).
2. Lobbying or political payment under §162(e). [Exceptions exist for payments to influence local legislation, §162(e)(2), for taxpayers engaged in the business of influencing legislation on behalf of another person, §162(e)(5)(A), and for certain de minimis in-house costs, §162(e)(5)(B).]
3. Fine or similar penalty to a government for violation of any law. *§162(f)*
4. Treble damage payment under antitrust law. *§162(g) (as to 2/3 of payment)*

Yes →

No ↓

Was the item an *expense* as opposed to a *capital expenditure*? See Map 7.5 — **No** →

Yes ↓

Was the expense "ordinary" (normal, usual, customary, expected in the life of the business)? *Welch v. Helvering* — **No** →

Yes ↓

Was the expense "necessary" (appropriate and helpful)? *Welch v. Helvering* — **No** →

Yes ↓

Was the expense paid or incurred "in carrying on any trade or business"? To be engaged in a trade or business:
1. Taxpayer must be involved in the activity with continuity and regularity; and
2. Taxpayer's primary purpose for engaging in the activity must be for income or profit. *Comm'r v. Groetzinger.* See Map 9.0

No →

47

Yes ↓

Was the expense paid or incurred in connection with any of the following?:
1. Investigating the creation or acquisition of an active trade or business; or
2. Creating an active trade or business; or
3. Engaging in any activity for profit and for production of income before the day on which the active trade or business begins, in anticipation of such activity becoming an active trade or business? *§195(c)*

No →

Yes ↓

Did taxpayer elect under §195 to deduct such start-up costs? *§195(b)* — **No** →

Yes ↓

Expense is currently deductible under §162.

Up to $5,000 of start-up expenses are deductible in the year in which the active trade or business begins, with the remainder deducted ratably over 180 months beginning with the month in which the active business begins. *§195*

Expense is not currently deductible under §162.

Common Examples of Ordinary & Necessary Business Expenses
- Reasonable salaries. *§162(a)(1)*. But see §162(m).
- Business travel expenses. *§162(a)(2)*. See Map 7.2
- Rent or royalties for use of property. *§162(a)(3)*
- Materials and supplies. *§1.162-3*
- Incidental repairs. *§1.162-4*
- Business education expenses. *§1.162-5*. See Map 7.1
- Specialty business attire. *Pevsner v. Comm'r*

Common Examples of Start-up Expenses
- Seeking and reviewing prospective businesses
- Employee training
- Lining up distributors, suppliers, and potential customers
- Setting up books and records

Notes

48

Business Education Expenses
7.1

Premise
This Map shows requirements that must be met in order for education expenses to be deductible as ordinary and necessary business expenses under §162.

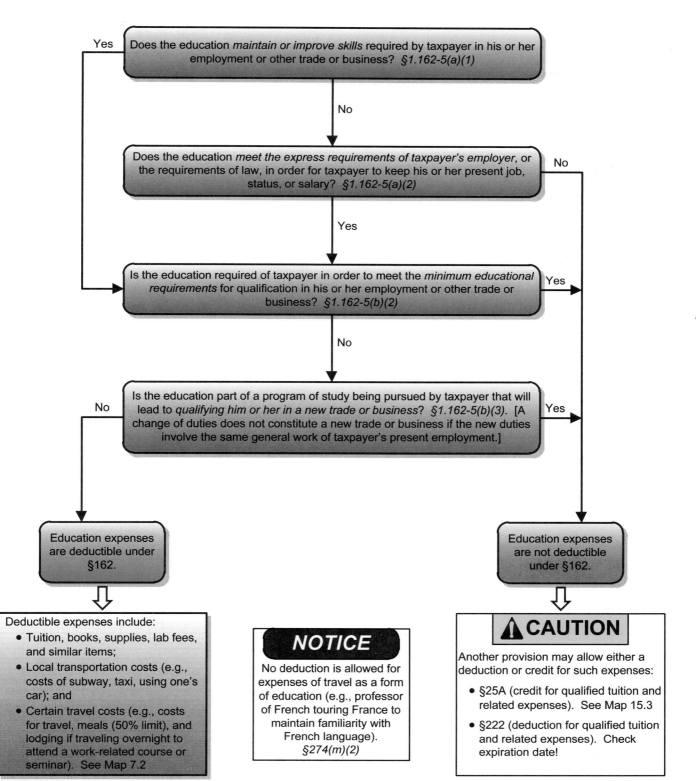

Yes — Does the education *maintain or improve skills* required by taxpayer in his or her employment or other trade or business? *§1.162-5(a)(1)*

No ↓

Does the education *meet the express requirements of taxpayer's employer*, or the requirements of law, in order for taxpayer to keep his or her present job, status, or salary? *§1.162-5(a)(2)* — No

Yes ↓

Is the education required of taxpayer in order to meet the *minimum educational requirements* for qualification in his or her employment or other trade or business? *§1.162-5(b)(2)* — Yes

No ↓

No — Is the education part of a program of study being pursued by taxpayer that will lead to *qualifying him or her in a new trade or business*? *§1.162-5(b)(3)*. [A change of duties does not constitute a new trade or business if the new duties involve the same general work of taxpayer's present employment.] — Yes

Education expenses are deductible under §162.

Education expenses are not deductible under §162.

Deductible expenses include:
- Tuition, books, supplies, lab fees, and similar items;
- Local transportation costs (e.g., costs of subway, taxi, using one's car); and
- Certain travel costs (e.g., costs for travel, meals (50% limit), and lodging if traveling overnight to attend a work-related course or seminar). See Map 7.2

NOTICE
No deduction is allowed for expenses of travel as a form of education (e.g., professor of French touring France to maintain familiarity with French language). *§274(m)(2)*

⚠ CAUTION
Another provision may allow either a deduction or credit for such expenses:
- §25A (credit for qualified tuition and related expenses). See Map 15.3
- §222 (deduction for qualified tuition and related expenses). Check expiration date!

49

Notes

Business Travel Expenses
7.2

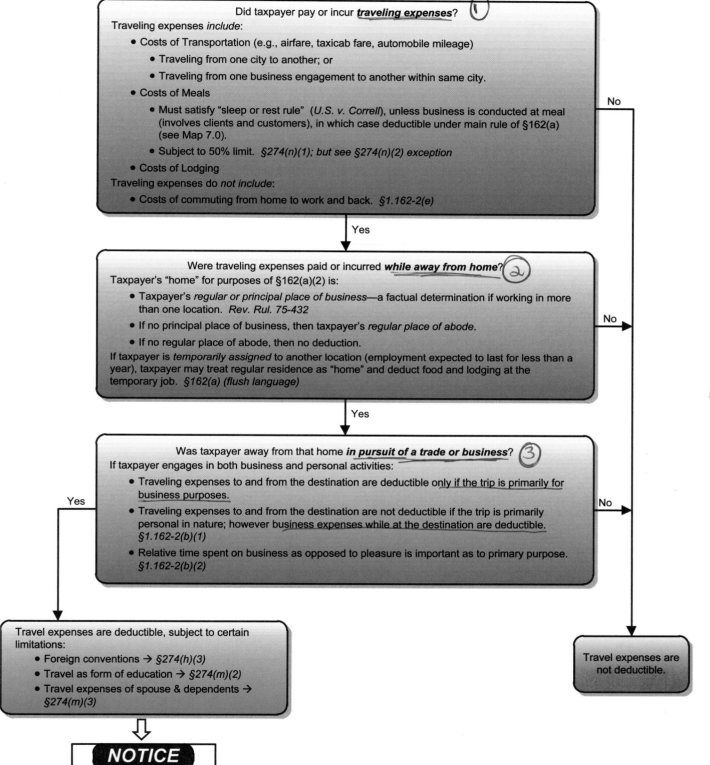

Did taxpayer pay or incur **_traveling expenses_**? ①

Traveling expenses *include*:

- Costs of Transportation (e.g., airfare, taxicab fare, automobile mileage)
    - Traveling from one city to another; or
    - Traveling from one business engagement to another within same city.
- Costs of Meals
    - Must satisfy "sleep or rest rule" (*U.S. v. Correll*), unless business is conducted at meal (involves clients and customers), in which case deductible under main rule of §162(a) (see Map 7.0).
    - Subject to 50% limit. *§274(n)(1); but see §274(n)(2) exception*
- Costs of Lodging

Traveling expenses do *not include*:

- Costs of commuting from home to work and back. *§1.162-2(e)*

No →

↓ **Yes**

Were traveling expenses paid or incurred **_while away from home_**? ②

Taxpayer's "home" for purposes of §162(a)(2) is:

- Taxpayer's *regular or principal place of business*—a factual determination if working in more than one location. *Rev. Rul. 75-432*
- If no principal place of business, then taxpayer's *regular place of abode*.
- If no regular place of abode, then no deduction.

If taxpayer is *temporarily assigned* to another location (employment expected to last for less than a year), taxpayer may treat regular residence as "home" and deduct food and lodging at the temporary job. *§162(a) (flush language)*

No →

↓ **Yes**

Was taxpayer away from that home **_in pursuit of a trade or business_**? ③

If taxpayer engages in both business and personal activities:

- Traveling expenses to and from the destination are deductible only if the trip is primarily for business purposes.
- Traveling expenses to and from the destination are not deductible if the trip is primarily personal in nature; however business expenses while at the destination are deductible. *§1.162-2(b)(1)*
- Relative time spent on business as opposed to pleasure is important as to primary purpose. *§1.162-2(b)(2)*

Yes ↓   **No** →

Travel expenses are deductible, subject to certain limitations:

- Foreign conventions → *§274(h)(3)*
- Travel as form of education → *§274(m)(2)*
- Travel expenses of spouse & dependents → *§274(m)(3)*

↓

NOTICE

Taxpayer must substantiate travel expenses. *§274(d)(1); §1.274-5T*

Travel expenses are not deductible.

51

Notes

Other Business Deductions
7.3 - Part 1

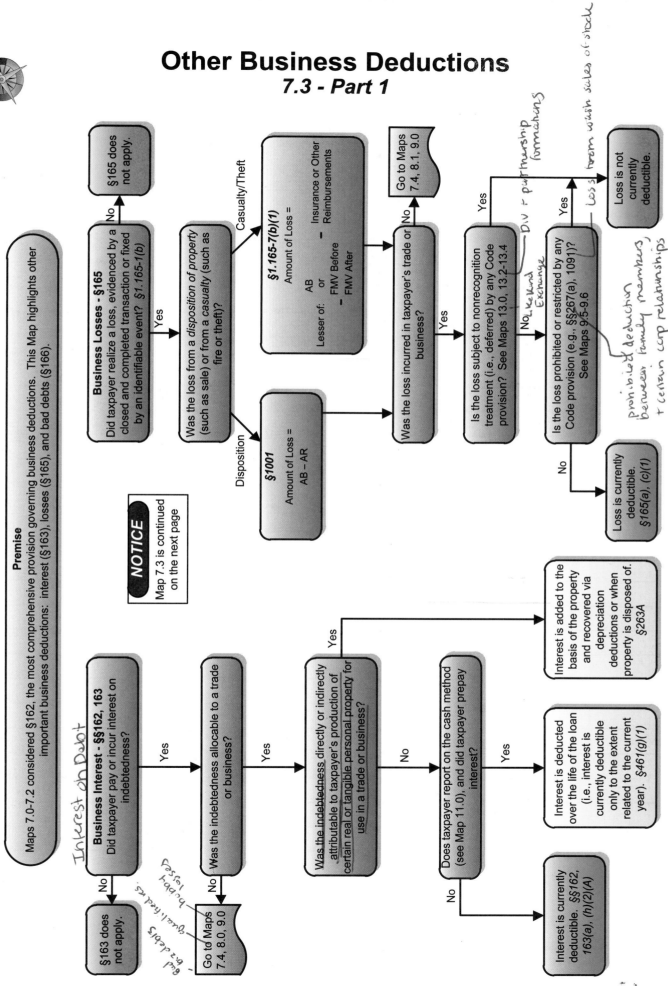

Premise

Maps 7.0-7.2 considered §162, the most comprehensive provision governing business deductions. This Map highlights other important business deductions: interest (§163), losses (§165), and bad debts (§166).

Business Losses - §165
Did taxpayer realize a loss, evidenced by a closed and completed transaction or fixed by an identifiable event? §1.165-1(b)

No → §165 does not apply.

Yes ↓

Was the loss from a *disposition* of property (such as sale) or from a *casualty* (such as fire or theft)?

Casualty/Theft →

§1.165-7(b)(1)
Amount of Loss =

Lesser of:
AB
or
FMV Before − FMV After

− Insurance or Other Reimbursements

Disposition →

§1001
Amount of Loss =
AB − AR

Was the loss incurred in taxpayer's trade or business?

No → Go to Maps 7.4, 8.1, 9.0

Yes → Is the loss subject to nonrecognition treatment (i.e., deferred) by any Code provision? See Maps 13.0, 13.2-13.4

Yes → (Like-kind Exchange; Div. & partnership formations)

No → Is the loss prohibited or restricted by any Code provision (e.g., §§267(a), 1091)? See Maps 9.5-9.6

Yes → Loss is not currently deductible. *(loss from w/sh sales of stock; prohibited deduction between family members + certain corp relationships)*

No → Loss is currently deductible. §165(a), (c)(1)

NOTICE
Map 7.3 is continued on the next page

Interest on Debt

Business Interest - §§162, 163
Did taxpayer pay or incur interest on indebtedness?

No → §163 does not apply.
(Bad debts → Qualified debts → bad debt losses)

Yes ↓

Was the indebtedness allocable to a trade or business?

No → Go to Maps 7.4, 8.0, 9.0

Yes ↓

Was the indebtedness directly or indirectly attributable to taxpayer's production of certain real or tangible personal property for use in a trade or business?

Yes → Interest is added to the basis of the property and recovered via depreciation deductions or when property is disposed of. §263A

No ↓

Does taxpayer report on the cash method (see Map 11.0), and did taxpayer prepay interest?

Yes → Interest is deducted over the life of the loan (i.e., interest is currently deductible only to the extent related to the current year). §461(g)(1)

No → Interest is currently deductible. §§162, 163(a), (h)(2)(A)

53

Notes

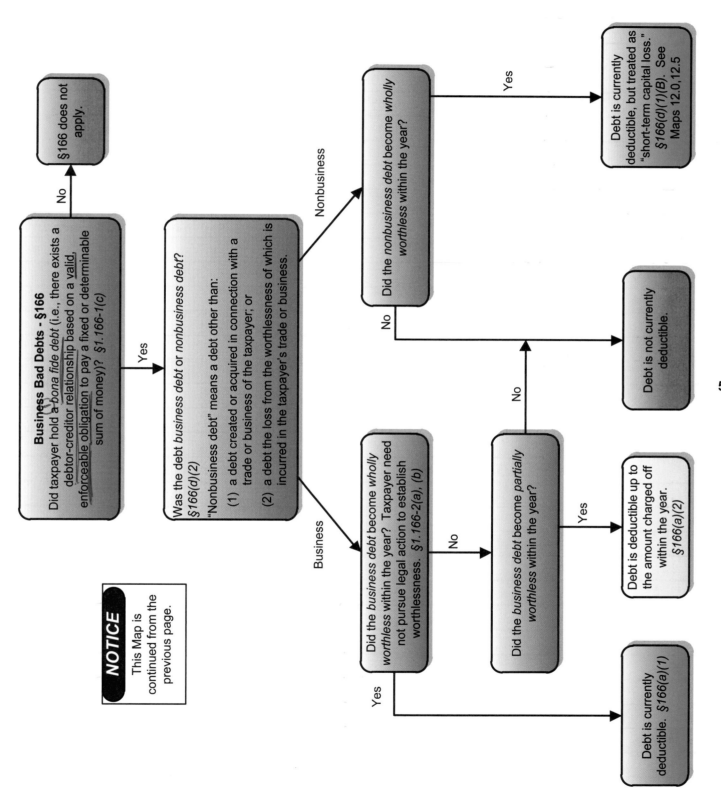

Business Bad Debts - §166

Did taxpayer hold a *bona fide debt* (i.e., there exists a debtor-creditor relationship based on a valid, enforceable obligation to pay a fixed or determinable sum of money)? *§1.166-1(c)*

No → §166 does not apply.

Yes ↓

Was the debt *business debt or nonbusiness debt*? *§166(d)(2)*

"Nonbusiness debt" means a debt other than:

(1) a debt created or acquired in connection with a trade or business of the taxpayer; or

(2) a debt the loss from the worthlessness of which is incurred in the taxpayer's trade or business.

Nonbusiness → Did the *nonbusiness debt* become *wholly worthless* within the year?

Yes → Debt is currently deductible, but treated as "short-term capital loss." *§166(d)(1)(B).* See Maps 12.0, 12.5

No → Debt is not currently deductible.

Business → Did the *business debt* become *wholly worthless* within the year? Taxpayer need not pursue legal action to establish worthlessness. *§1.166-2(a), (b)*

Yes → Debt is currently deductible. *§166(a)(1)*

No → Did the *business debt* become *partially worthless* within the year?

Yes → Debt is deductible up to the amount charged off within the year. *§166(a)(2)*

No → Debt is not currently deductible.

NOTICE

This Map is continued from the previous page.

55

Notes

Section 212: Expenses for Production of Income
7.4

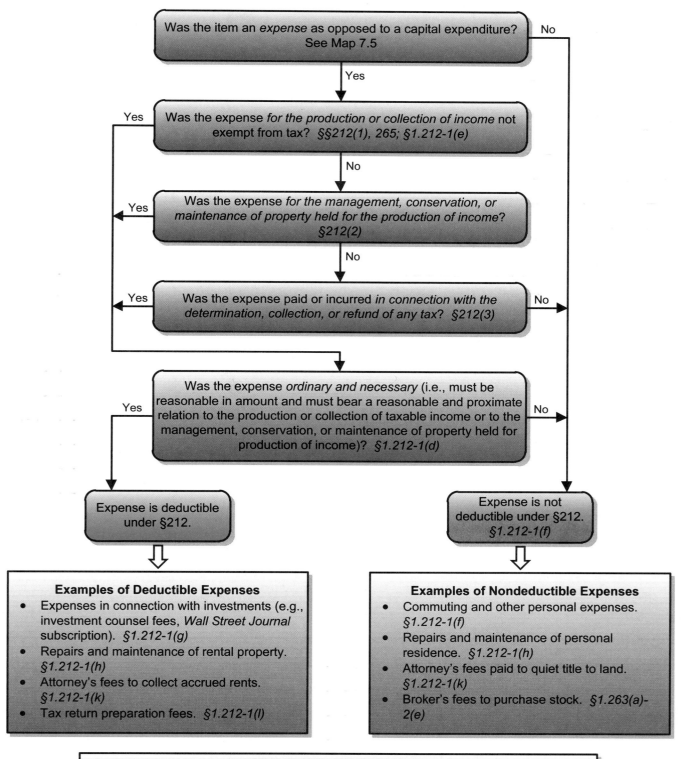

Was the item an *expense* as opposed to a capital expenditure? See Map 7.5 — No →

Yes ↓

Was the expense *for the production or collection of income* not exempt from tax? *§§212(1), 265; §1.212-1(e)* — Yes ←

No ↓

Was the expense *for the management, conservation, or maintenance of property held for the production of income*? *§212(2)* — Yes ←

No ↓

Was the expense paid or incurred *in connection with the determination, collection, or refund of any tax*? *§212(3)* — Yes ← / No →

Was the expense *ordinary and necessary* (i.e., must be reasonable in amount and must bear a reasonable and proximate relation to the production or collection of taxable income or to the management, conservation, or maintenance of property held for production of income)? *§1.212-1(d)* — Yes ← / No →

Expense is deductible under §212.

Expense is not deductible under §212. *§1.212-1(f)*

Examples of Deductible Expenses
- Expenses in connection with investments (e.g., investment counsel fees, *Wall Street Journal* subscription). *§1.212-1(g)*
- Repairs and maintenance of rental property. *§1.212-1(h)*
- Attorney's fees to collect accrued rents. *§1.212-1(k)*
- Tax return preparation fees. *§1.212-1(l)*

Examples of Nondeductible Expenses
- Commuting and other personal expenses. *§1.212-1(f)*
- Repairs and maintenance of personal residence. *§1.212-1(h)*
- Attorney's fees paid to quiet title to land. *§1.212-1(k)*
- Broker's fees to purchase stock. *§1.263(a)-2(e)*

Other Investment Deductions
- Investment interest to the extent of "net investment income." *§163(a), (h)(2)(B), (d)*
- Losses incurred in any transaction entered into for profit, though not connected with a trade or business. *§165(a), (c)(2)*
- Depreciation of property held for the production of income. *§167(a)(2)*. See Maps 7.6-7.7

Notes

58

Nondeductible Capital Expenditures
7.5

Y

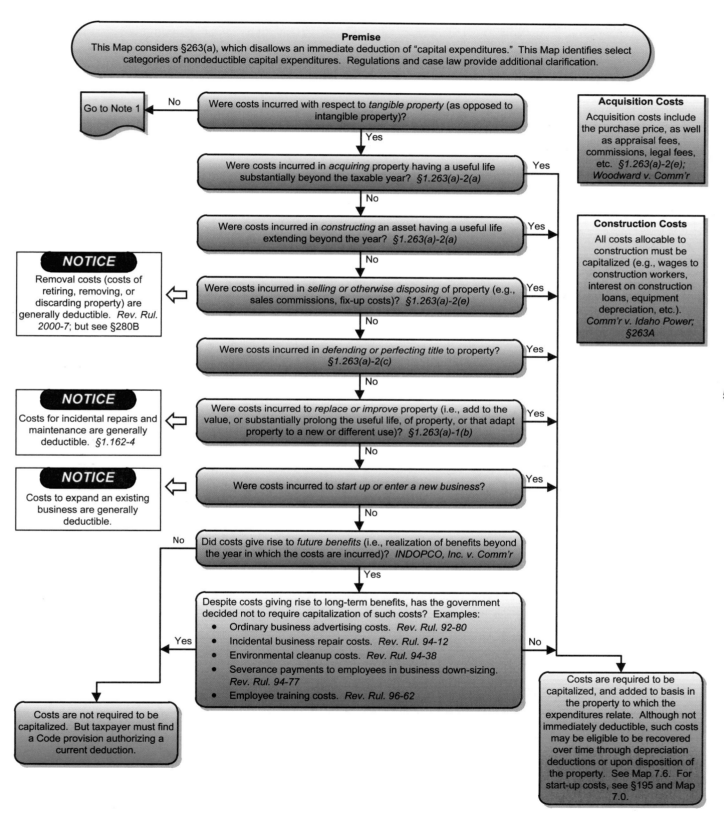

Premise
This Map considers §263(a), which disallows an immediate deduction of "capital expenditures." This Map identifies select categories of nondeductible capital expenditures. Regulations and case law provide additional clarification.

Go to Note 1 ← No — Were costs incurred with respect to *tangible property* (as opposed to intangible property)?
Yes

Were costs incurred in *acquiring* property having a useful life substantially beyond the taxable year? *§1.263(a)-2(a)* — Yes →
No

Were costs incurred in *constructing* an asset having a useful life extending beyond the year? *§1.263(a)-2(a)* — Yes →
No

NOTICE
Removal costs (costs of retiring, removing, or discarding property) are generally deductible. *Rev. Rul. 2000-7*; but see §280B

← Were costs incurred in *selling or otherwise disposing* of property (e.g., sales commissions, fix-up costs)? *§1.263(a)-2(e)* — Yes →
No

Were costs incurred in *defending or perfecting title* to property? *§1.263(a)-2(c)* — Yes →
No

NOTICE
Costs for incidental repairs and maintenance are generally deductible. *§1.162-4*

← Were costs incurred to *replace or improve* property (i.e., add to the value, or substantially prolong the useful life, of property, or that adapt property to a new or different use)? *§1.263(a)-1(b)* — Yes →
No

NOTICE
Costs to expand an existing business are generally deductible.

← Were costs incurred to *start up or enter a new business*? — Yes →
No

No ← Did costs give rise to *future benefits* (i.e., realization of benefits beyond the year in which the costs are incurred)? *INDOPCO, Inc. v. Comm'r*
Yes

Despite costs giving rise to long-term benefits, has the government decided not to require capitalization of such costs? Examples:
- Ordinary business advertising costs. *Rev. Rul. 92-80*
- Incidental business repair costs. *Rev. Rul. 94-12*
- Environmental cleanup costs. *Rev. Rul. 94-38*
- Severance payments to employees in business down-sizing. *Rev. Rul. 94-77*
- Employee training costs. *Rev. Rul. 96-62*

Yes (left) / No (right)

Acquisition Costs
Acquisition costs include the purchase price, as well as appraisal fees, commissions, legal fees, etc. *§1.263(a)-2(e); Woodward v. Comm'r*

Construction Costs
All costs allocable to construction must be capitalized (e.g., wages to construction workers, interest on construction loans, equipment depreciation, etc.). *Comm'r v. Idaho Power; §263A*

Costs are not required to be capitalized. But taxpayer must find a Code provision authorizing a current deduction.

Costs are required to be capitalized, and added to basis in the property to which the expenditures relate. Although not immediately deductible, such costs may be eligible to be recovered over time through depreciation deductions or upon disposition of the property. See Map 7.6. For start-up costs, see §195 and Map 7.0.

59

60

Nondeductible Capital Expenditures
7.5 Notes

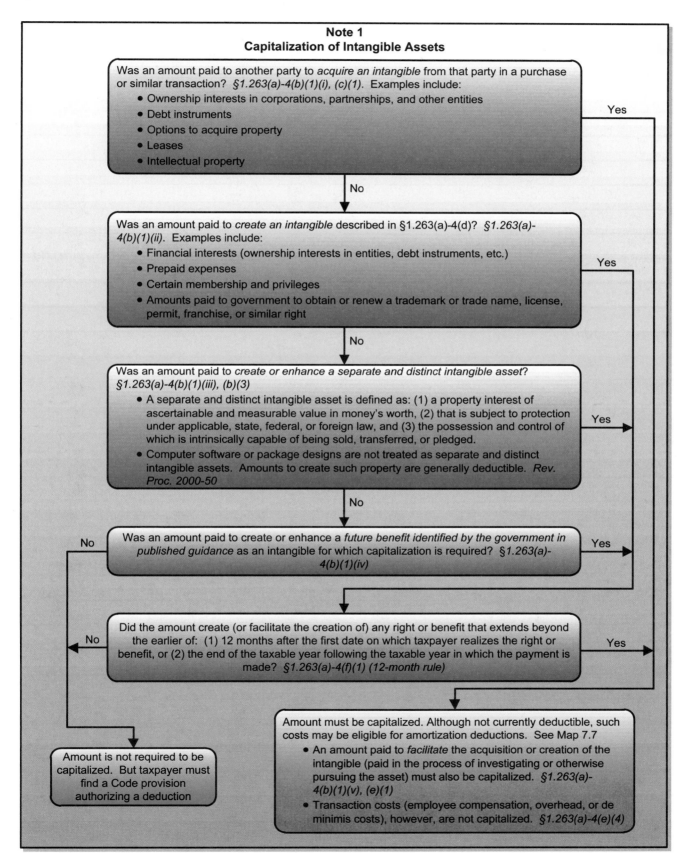

Note 1
Capitalization of Intangible Assets

Was an amount paid to another party to *acquire an intangible* from that party in a purchase or similar transaction? *§1.263(a)-4(b)(1)(i), (c)(1)*. Examples include:
- Ownership interests in corporations, partnerships, and other entities
- Debt instruments
- Options to acquire property
- Leases
- Intellectual property

→ Yes

↓ No

Was an amount paid to *create an intangible* described in §1.263(a)-4(d)? *§1.263(a)-4(b)(1)(ii)*. Examples include:
- Financial interests (ownership interests in entities, debt instruments, etc.)
- Prepaid expenses
- Certain membership and privileges
- Amounts paid to government to obtain or renew a trademark or trade name, license, permit, franchise, or similar right

→ Yes

↓ No

Was an amount paid to *create or enhance a separate and distinct intangible asset*? *§1.263(a)-4(b)(1)(iii), (b)(3)*
- A separate and distinct intangible asset is defined as: (1) a property interest of ascertainable and measurable value in money's worth, (2) that is subject to protection under applicable, state, federal, or foreign law, and (3) the possession and control of which is intrinsically capable of being sold, transferred, or pledged.
- Computer software or package designs are not treated as separate and distinct intangible assets. Amounts to create such property are generally deductible. *Rev. Proc. 2000-50*

→ Yes

↓ No

Was an amount paid to create or enhance a *future benefit identified by the government in published guidance* as an intangible for which capitalization is required? *§1.263(a)-4(b)(1)(iv)*

No ← | → Yes

↓

Did the amount create (or facilitate the creation of) any right or benefit that extends beyond the earlier of: (1) 12 months after the first date on which taxpayer realizes the right or benefit, or (2) the end of the taxable year following the taxable year in which the payment is made? *§1.263(a)-4(f)(1) (12-month rule)*

No ← | → Yes

Amount is not required to be capitalized. But taxpayer must find a Code provision authorizing a deduction

Amount must be capitalized. Although not currently deductible, such costs may be eligible for amortization deductions. See Map 7.7
- An amount paid to *facilitate* the acquisition or creation of the intangible (paid in the process of investigating or otherwise pursuing the asset) must also be capitalized. *§1.263(a)-4(b)(1)(v), (e)(1)*
- Transaction costs (employee compensation, overhead, or de minimis costs), however, are not capitalized. *§1.263(a)-4(e)(4)*

61

Notes

Depreciation of Tangible Property
7.6

[handwritten: Must be used in trade or biz + wear + tear]

Is the property *tangible* property? — No → **Go to Map 7.7**

Yes ↓

Is the tangible property subject to *wear and tear*? *Simon v. Comm'r* — No →

Yes ↓

Is the tangible property either used in *trade or business* or held for *production of income*? — No → **No depreciation deduction is allowed.**

Yes ↓

This Map highlights key tax depreciation rules. There are many nuances to tax depreciation not touched upon here.

Is the tangible property *personal* property (e.g., equipment) OR *real* property (apartment or office building)? — Real Property →

Personal Property ↓

[handwritten: §179]

Is the property "§179 property" (i.e., tangible *personal* property *purchased* for *active* conduct of *trade or business*)? *§§179(d)(1), 1245(a)(3)* — No →

Yes ↓

Did taxpayer *elect* to deduct currently the cost of the §179 property (treat as an *expense* as opposed to a capital expenditure)? *§179(a)* — No →

Yes ↓

⚠ CAUTION
- There are limits on the amount that can be expensed in any given year: *§179(b)(1)* (dollar limit), *(b)(2)* (investment limit), *(b)(3)* (taxable income limit).
- Adjusted basis is reduced by the amount of the §179 expense deduction before moving to the next step.

(if AB is remaining) ⇩

Is the property "qualified property" eligible for §168(k) *bonus depreciation* (e.g., *new*, depreciable tangible personal property)? — No →

Yes ↓

Did taxpayer elect out of the 50% bonus depreciation? *168(k)(2)(D)(iii)* — Yes →

No ↓

⚠ CAUTION
- §168(k) has been enacted several times on a *temporary* basis to provide an extra up-front depreciation deduction (50% in year of acquisition) for qualified property.
- Adjusted basis is reduced by the bonus depreciation before moving to the next step.

(if AB is remaining) ⇩

Did taxpayer elect to use the alternative depreciation system? *§168(g)*

No ← → Yes

Accelerated Cost Recovery System (ACRS)
Depreciation deduction is determined using:
1. applicable depreciation method *§168(b)*
2. applicable recovery period *§168(c), (e)*
3. applicable convention *§168(d)*

Alternative Depreciation System
Depreciation deduction is determined using:
1. straight line method *§168(g)(2)(A)*
2. applicable convention *§168(g)(2)(B), (d)*
3. class life recovery period for personal property *§168(g)(2)(C)(i)*
4. 40-year recovery period for real property *§168(g)(2)(C)(iii)*

⚠ CAUTION
- Depreciation is allowed only on that portion of the property that is used in a trade or business or for the production of income. *Sharp v. U.S.*
- Aggregate depreciation is limited to adjusted basis in the property. *§167(c)*. If property is converted from personal use to business use, basis for depreciation purposes cannot exceed FMV of property at time of conversion. *§1.167(g)-1*
- Basis in depreciable property must be reduced by the greater of the amount allowed (claimed) or allowable (could have been claimed). *§1016(a)(2)*
- For limits on depreciation deductions on personal residences that are partly used for business or are rented as vacation homes, see §280A. See Maps 9.3-9.4
- For limits on depreciation deductions on luxury automobiles and mixed-use personal property, see §280F.

63

Notes

64

Amortization of Intangible Property
7.7

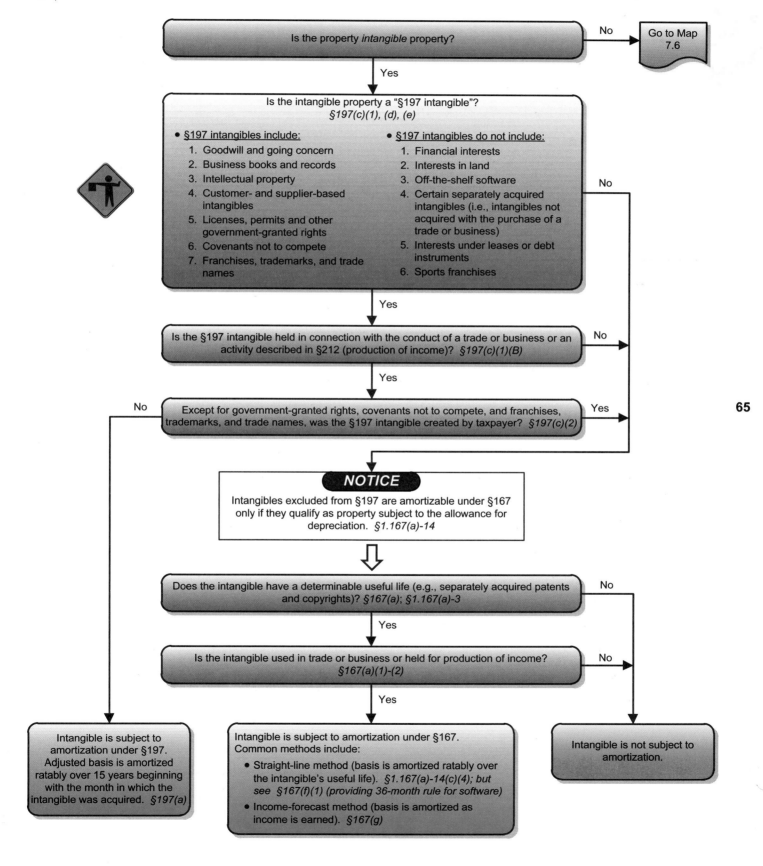

Is the property *intangible* property? — No → Go to Map 7.6

Yes ↓

Is the intangible property a "§197 intangible"?
§197(c)(1), (d), (e)

- §197 intangibles include:
  1. Goodwill and going concern
  2. Business books and records
  3. Intellectual property
  4. Customer- and supplier-based intangibles
  5. Licenses, permits and other government-granted rights
  6. Covenants not to compete
  7. Franchises, trademarks, and trade names

- §197 intangibles do not include:
  1. Financial interests
  2. Interests in land
  3. Off-the-shelf software
  4. Certain separately acquired intangibles (i.e., intangibles not acquired with the purchase of a trade or business)
  5. Interests under leases or debt instruments
  6. Sports franchises

No →

Yes ↓

Is the §197 intangible held in connection with the conduct of a trade or business or an activity described in §212 (production of income)? *§197(c)(1)(B)* — No →

Yes ↓

No ← **Except for government-granted rights, covenants not to compete, and franchises, trademarks, and trade names, was the §197 intangible created by taxpayer?** *§197(c)(2)* — Yes →

↓

NOTICE

Intangibles excluded from §197 are amortizable under §167 only if they qualify as property subject to the allowance for depreciation. *§1.167(a)-14*

⇩

Does the intangible have a determinable useful life (e.g., separately acquired patents and copyrights)? *§167(a); §1.167(a)-3* — No →

Yes ↓

Is the intangible used in trade or business or held for production of income? *§167(a)(1)-(2)* — No →

Yes ↓

Intangible is subject to amortization under §197. Adjusted basis is amortized ratably over 15 years beginning with the month in which the intangible was acquired. *§197(a)*

Intangible is subject to amortization under §167. Common methods include:

- Straight-line method (basis is amortized ratably over the intangible's useful life). *§1.167(a)-14(c)(4); but see §167(f)(1) (providing 36-month rule for software)*
- Income-forecast method (basis is amortized as income is earned). *§167(g)*

Intangible is not subject to amortization.

Notes

Qualified Residence Interest
8.0

(Mortgage Interest)

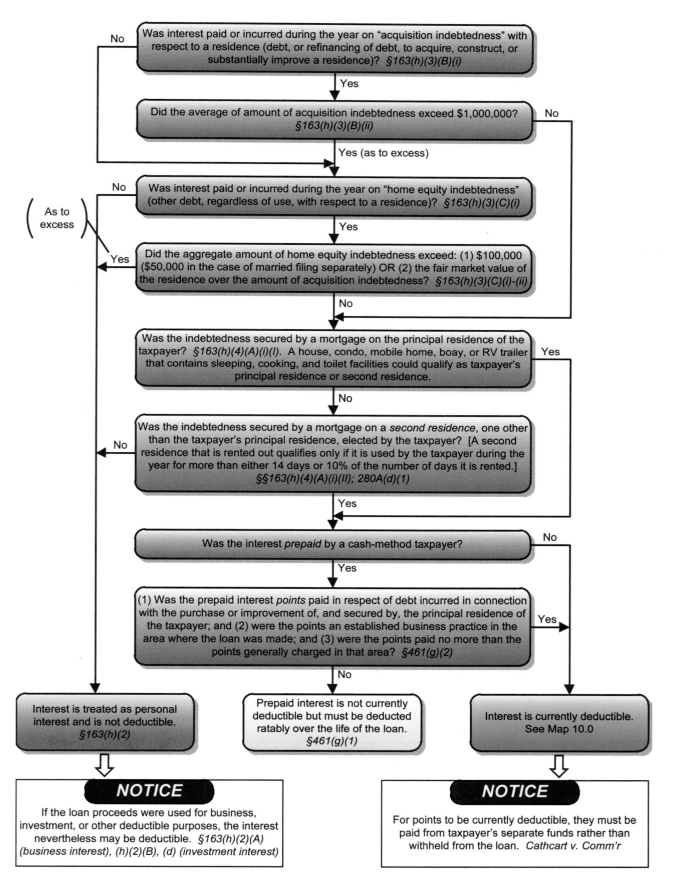

Was interest paid or incurred during the year on "acquisition indebtedness" with respect to a residence (debt, or refinancing of debt, to acquire, construct, or substantially improve a residence)? *§163(h)(3)(B)(i)* — **No** / **Yes**

Did the average of amount of acquisition indebtedness exceed $1,000,000? *§163(h)(3)(B)(ii)* — **No** / **Yes (as to excess)**

Was interest paid or incurred during the year on "home equity indebtedness" (other debt, regardless of use, with respect to a residence)? *§163(h)(3)(C)(i)* — **No** / **Yes**

Did the aggregate amount of home equity indebtedness exceed: (1) $100,000 ($50,000 in the case of married filing separately) OR (2) the fair market value of the residence over the amount of acquisition indebtedness? *§163(h)(3)(C)(i)-(ii)* — **Yes** / **No**

(As to excess)

Was the indebtedness secured by a mortgage on the principal residence of the taxpayer? *§163(h)(4)(A)(i)(I)*. A house, condo, mobile home, boay, or RV trailer that contains sleeping, cooking, and toilet facilities could qualify as taxpayer's principal residence or second residence. — **Yes** / **No**

Was the indebtedness secured by a mortgage on a *second residence*, one other than the taxpayer's principal residence, elected by the taxpayer? [A second residence that is rented out qualifies only if it is used by the taxpayer during the year for more than either 14 days or 10% of the number of days it is rented.] *§§163(h)(4)(A)(i)(II); 280A(d)(1)* — **No** / **Yes**

Was the interest *prepaid* by a cash-method taxpayer? — **No** / **Yes**

(1) Was the prepaid interest *points* paid in respect of debt incurred in connection with the purchase or improvement of, and secured by, the principal residence of the taxpayer; and (2) were the points an established business practice in the area where the loan was made; and (3) were the points paid no more than the points generally charged in that area? *§461(g)(2)* — **Yes** / **No**

Interest is treated as personal interest and is not deductible. *§163(h)(2)*

Prepaid interest is not currently deductible but must be deducted ratably over the life of the loan. *§461(g)(1)*

Interest is currently deductible. See Map 10.0

NOTICE
If the loan proceeds were used for business, investment, or other deductible purposes, the interest nevertheless may be deductible. *§163(h)(2)(A) (business interest), (h)(2)(B), (d) (investment interest)*

NOTICE
For points to be currently deductible, they must be paid from taxpayer's separate funds rather than withheld from the loan. *Cathcart v. Comm'r*

Notes

Casualty Losses
8.1

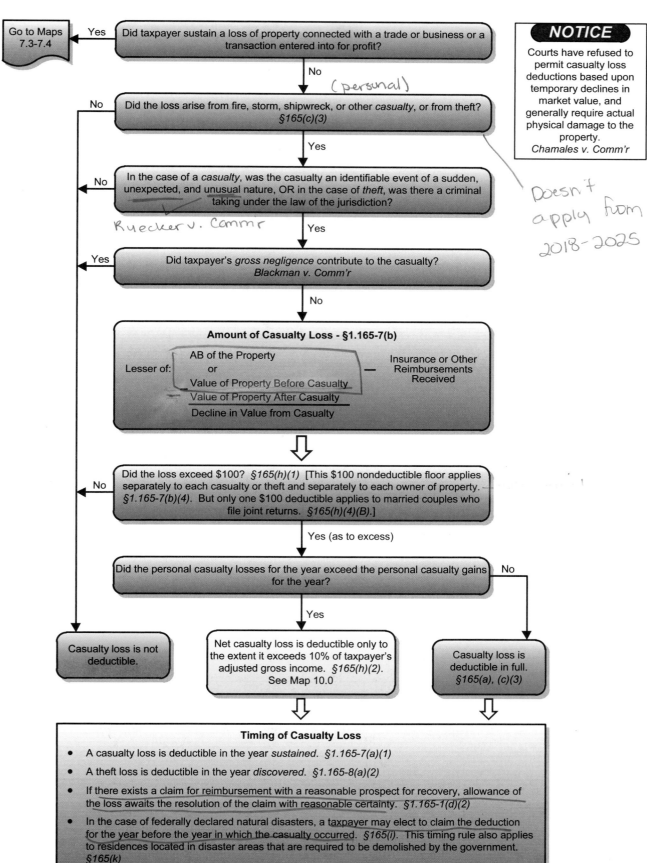

Y

Did taxpayer sustain a loss of property connected with a trade or business or a transaction entered into for profit? — Yes → **Go to Maps 7.3-7.4**

No ↓ *(personal)*

Did the loss arise from fire, storm, shipwreck, or other *casualty*, or from theft? §165(c)(3) — No →

Yes ↓

In the case of a *casualty*, was the casualty an identifiable event of a sudden, unexpected, and unusual nature, OR in the case of *theft*, was there a criminal taking under the law of the jurisdiction? — No →

Ruecker v. Comm'r

Yes ↓

Did taxpayer's *gross negligence* contribute to the casualty?
Blackman v. Comm'r — Yes →

No ↓

Amount of Casualty Loss - §1.165-7(b)

Lesser of: { AB of the Property or Value of Property Before Casualty } − Value of Property After Casualty = Decline in Value from Casualty − Insurance or Other Reimbursements Received

⇩

Did the loss exceed $100? *§165(h)(1)* [This $100 nondeductible floor applies separately to each casualty or theft and separately to each owner of property. *§1.165-7(b)(4)*. But only one $100 deductible applies to married couples who file joint returns. *§165(h)(4)(B)*.] — No →

Yes (as to excess) ↓

Did the personal casualty losses for the year exceed the personal casualty gains for the year? — No →

Yes ↓

Casualty loss is not deductible.

Net casualty loss is deductible only to the extent it exceeds 10% of taxpayer's adjusted gross income. *§165(h)(2)*. See Map 10.0

Casualty loss is deductible in full. *§165(a), (c)(3)*

⇩ ⇩

Timing of Casualty Loss

- A casualty loss is deductible in the year *sustained*. *§1.165-7(a)(1)*
- A theft loss is deductible in the year *discovered*. *§1.165-8(a)(2)*
- If there exists a claim for reimbursement with a reasonable prospect for recovery, allowance of the loss awaits the resolution of the claim with reasonable certainty. *§1.165-1(d)(2)*
- In the case of federally declared natural disasters, a taxpayer may elect to claim the deduction for the year before the year in which the casualty occurred. *§165(i)*. This timing rule also applies to residences located in disaster areas that are required to be demolished by the government. *§165(k)*

NOTICE
Courts have refused to permit casualty loss deductions based upon temporary declines in market value, and generally require actual physical damage to the property.
Chamales v. Comm'r

Doesn't apply from 2018-2025

69

Notes

70

Charitable Contributions
8.2

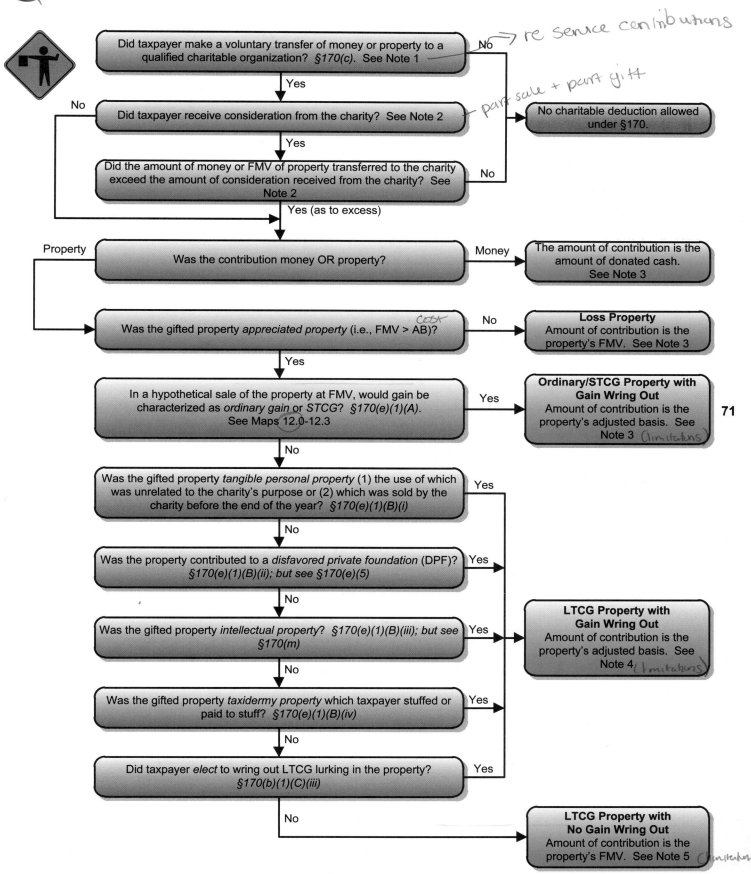

Y

→ re service contributions

Did taxpayer make a voluntary transfer of money or property to a qualified charitable organization? §170(c). See Note 1 — **No** →

← part sale + part gift

Did taxpayer receive consideration from the charity? See Note 2 — **No** →

No charitable deduction allowed under §170.

Did the amount of money or FMV of property transferred to the charity exceed the amount of consideration received from the charity? See Note 2 — **No** →

Yes ↓ / **Yes** ↓ / **Yes (as to excess)** ↓

Was the contribution money OR property? — **Money** →

The amount of contribution is the amount of donated cash. See Note 3

Property ↓

Was the gifted property *appreciated property* (i.e., FMV > AB)? [cost] — **No** →

Loss Property
Amount of contribution is the property's FMV. See Note 3

Yes ↓

In a hypothetical sale of the property at FMV, would gain be characterized as *ordinary gain* or *STCG*? §170(e)(1)(A). See Maps 12.0-12.3 — **Yes** →

Ordinary/STCG Property with Gain Wring Out
Amount of contribution is the property's adjusted basis. See Note 3 (limitations)

71

No ↓

Was the gifted property *tangible personal property* (1) the use of which was unrelated to the charity's purpose or (2) which was sold by the charity before the end of the year? §170(e)(1)(B)(i) — **Yes** →

No ↓

Was the property contributed to a *disfavored private foundation* (DPF)? §170(e)(1)(B)(ii); but see §170(e)(5) — **Yes** →

No ↓

Was the gifted property *intellectual property*? §170(e)(1)(B)(iii); but see §170(m) — **Yes** →

LTCG Property with Gain Wring Out
Amount of contribution is the property's adjusted basis. See Note 4 (limitations)

No ↓

Was the gifted property *taxidermy property* which taxpayer stuffed or paid to stuff? §170(e)(1)(B)(iv) — **Yes** →

No ↓

Did taxpayer *elect* to wring out LTCG lurking in the property? §170(b)(1)(C)(iii) — **Yes** →

No ↓

LTCG Property with No Gain Wring Out
Amount of contribution is the property's FMV. See Note 5 (limitations)

Notes

72

Charitable Contributions
8.2 Notes

γ

Note 1
Service Contributions

- Services rendered to a charity do not qualify as charitable contributions. ✓
- Unreimbursed expenses incurred incident to rendering of such services may constitute charitable contributions. *§1.170A-1(g)*
- §170(i) allows a standard mileage rate for transportation costs.

Note 2
Quid Pro Quo Contributions

- If cash is given to a charity and partial consideration is received from the charity, only the excess of the amount of cash over the amount of consideration received qualifies as a charitable deduction.
- If property is transferred for partial consideration, a part sale-part gift occurs. The *sale* is treated under §1001 and the characterization rules, and the *gift* is treated under §170. Taxpayer has made a charitable gift to the extent value exceeds selling price. §1011(b) determines how much basis to allocate to the sale; the rest is allocated to the charitable gift. §1011(b) provides:

$$\frac{\text{Amount Realized}}{\text{Fair Market Value}} \quad \times \quad \text{Adjusted Basis} \quad = \quad \begin{array}{c}\text{Basis Allocated}\\\text{to Sale}\end{array}$$

AR - AB = Gain

Note 3
Limitations on Gifts of These Properties

73

- Contributions of this type property to *public charities* are deductible to the extent such contributions do not exceed 50% of the taxpayer's *contribution base* (CB). *§170(b)(1)(A)*. Any excess caries over for 5 years. *§170(d)(1)(A)*
- Contributions of this type property to *disfavored private foundations (DPFs)* are subject to a limitation of 30% of CB for the year. *§170(b)(1)(B)(i)*. But such contributions may not exceed 50% of the CB less the amount of property contributed to public charities. *§170(b)(1)(B)(ii)*. Any excess caries over 5 years. *§170(b)(1)(B) (flush language)*

CB = Adj. Gross Income

Note 4
Limitations on Gifts of These Properties

- Contributions of this type property to *public charities* are deductible to the extent such contributions do not exceed 50% of the contribution base (CB). *§170(b)(1)(A)*. Any excess caries over for up to 5 years. *§170(d)(1)(A)*
- Contributions of this type property to *disfavored private foundations (DPFs)* are subject to a ceiling of 20% of the CB, but not in excess of 30% of CB minus any unreduced LTCG property given to a public charity. *§170(b)(1)(D)(i)*. Any excess caries over for 5 years. *§170(b)(1)(D)(ii)*

* If over $250 need contemp. written ack. that nothing in return *

Note 5
Limitations on Gifts of These Properties

- Contributions of this type property to *public charities* are deductible to the extent such contributions do not exceed 30% of the taxpayer's contribution base (CB). *§170(b)(1)(C)(i)*. Any excess carries over for 5 years. *§170(b)(1)(C)(ii)*
- Contributions of this type property to *disfavored private foundations (DPFs)* are subject to a ceiling of 20% of the CB, but not in excess of 30% of CB minus any unreduced LTCG property given to a public charity. *§170(b)(1)(D)(i)*. Any excess caries over for 5 years. *§170(b)(1)(D)(ii)*

Notes

74

Medical Expenses
8.3

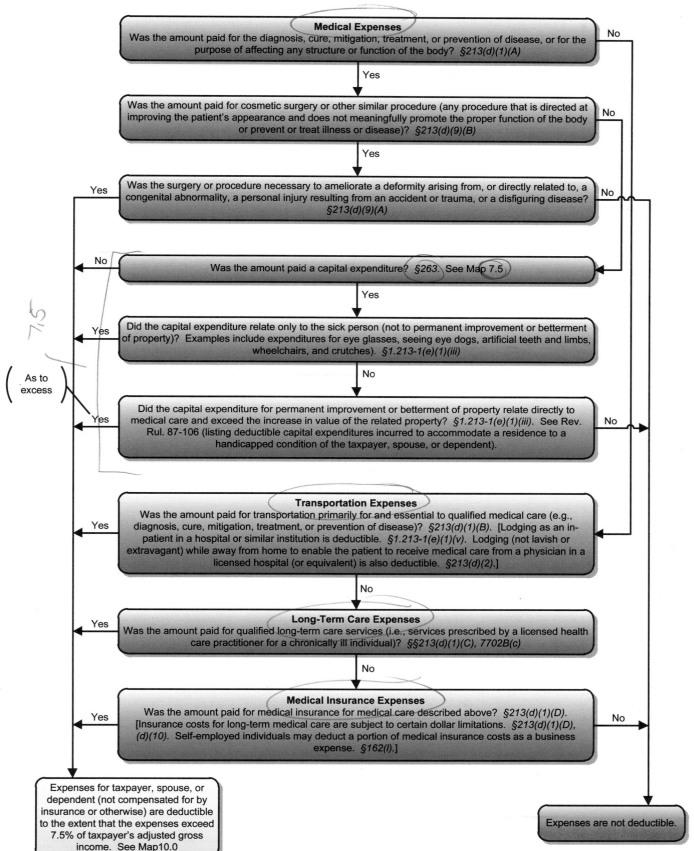

Medical Expenses
Was the amount paid for the diagnosis, cure, mitigation, treatment, or prevention of disease, or for the purpose of affecting any structure or function of the body? *§213(d)(1)(A)* — No

Yes

Was the amount paid for cosmetic surgery or other similar procedure (any procedure that is directed at improving the patient's appearance and does not meaningfully promote the proper function of the body or prevent or treat illness or disease)? *§213(d)(9)(B)* — No

Yes

Yes — Was the surgery or procedure necessary to ameliorate a deformity arising from, or directly related to, a congenital abnormality, a personal injury resulting from an accident or trauma, or a disfiguring disease? *§213(d)(9)(A)* — No

No — Was the amount paid a capital expenditure? *§263.* See Map 7.5

Yes

As to excess

Yes — Did the capital expenditure relate only to the sick person (not to permanent improvement or betterment of property)? Examples include expenditures for eye glasses, seeing eye dogs, artificial teeth and limbs, wheelchairs, and crutches). *§1.213-1(e)(1)(iii)*

No

Yes — Did the capital expenditure for permanent improvement or betterment of property relate directly to medical care and exceed the increase in value of the related property? *§1.213-1(e)(1)(iii).* See Rev. Rul. 87-106 (listing deductible capital expenditures incurred to accommodate a residence to a handicapped condition of the taxpayer, spouse, or dependent). — No

75

Transportation Expenses
Yes — Was the amount paid for transportation primarily for and essential to qualified medical care (e.g., diagnosis, cure, mitigation, treatment, or prevention of disease)? *§213(d)(1)(B).* [Lodging as an in-patient in a hospital or similar institution is deductible. *§1.213-1(e)(1)(v).* Lodging (not lavish or extravagant) while away from home to enable the patient to receive medical care from a physician in a licensed hospital (or equivalent) is also deductible. *§213(d)(2).*]

No

Long-Term Care Expenses
Yes — Was the amount paid for qualified long-term care services (i.e., services prescribed by a licensed health care practitioner for a chronically ill individual)? *§§213(d)(1)(C), 7702B(c)*

No

Medical Insurance Expenses
Yes — Was the amount paid for medical insurance for medical care described above? *§213(d)(1)(D).* [Insurance costs for long-term medical care are subject to certain dollar limitations. *§213(d)(1)(D), (d)(10).* Self-employed individuals may deduct a portion of medical insurance costs as a business expense. *§162(l).*] — No

Expenses for taxpayer, spouse, or dependent (not compensated for by insurance or otherwise) are deductible to the extent that the expenses exceed 7.5% of taxpayer's adjusted gross income. See Map10.0

Expenses are not deductible.

Notes

Alimony and Separate Maintenance Payments
8.4

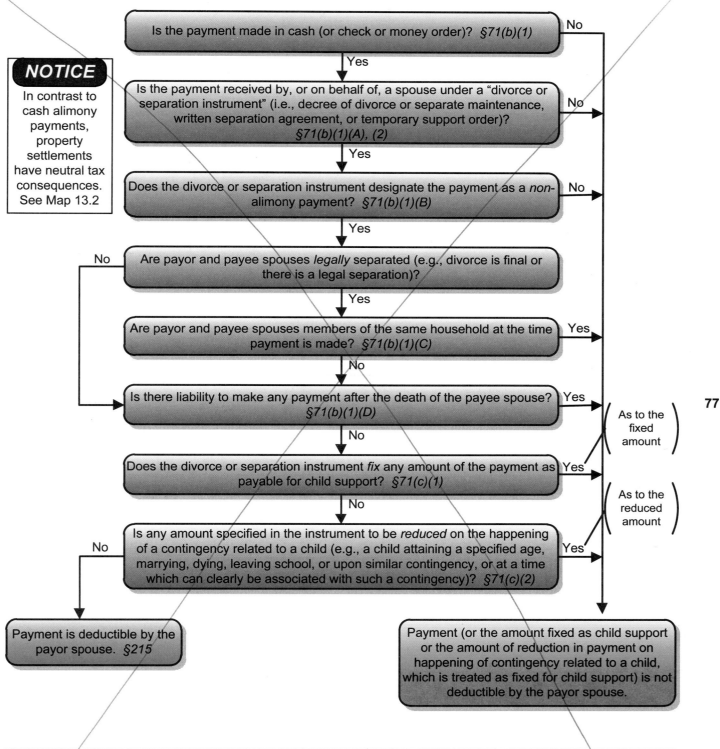

Is the payment made in cash (or check or money order)? *§71(b)(1)* — No →

Yes ↓

NOTICE

In contrast to cash alimony payments, property settlements have neutral tax consequences. See Map 13.2

Is the payment received by, or on behalf of, a spouse under a "divorce or separation instrument" (i.e., decree of divorce or separate maintenance, written separation agreement, or temporary support order)? *§71(b)(1)(A), (2)* — No →

Yes ↓

Does the divorce or separation instrument designate the payment as a *non-alimony* payment? *§71(b)(1)(B)* — No →

Yes ↓

No ← Are payor and payee spouses *legally* separated (e.g., divorce is final or there is a legal separation)?

Yes ↓

Are payor and payee spouses members of the same household at the time payment is made? *§71(b)(1)(C)* — Yes →

No ↓

Is there liability to make any payment after the death of the payee spouse? *§71(b)(1)(D)* — Yes →

77

As to the fixed amount

No ↓

Does the divorce or separation instrument *fix* any amount of the payment as payable for child support? *§71(c)(1)* — Yes →

No ↓

As to the reduced amount

No ← Is any amount specified in the instrument to be *reduced* on the happening of a contingency related to a child (e.g., a child attaining a specified age, marrying, dying, leaving school, or upon similar contingency, or at a time which can clearly be associated with such a contingency)? *§71(c)(2)* — Yes →

Payment is deductible by the payor spouse. *§215*

Payment (or the amount fixed as child support or the amount of reduction in payment on happening of contingency related to a child, which is treated as fixed for child support) is not deductible by the payor spouse.

Front-Loading of Alimony
(Disguised Property Settlements)

To discourage front-loading of alimony payments (early large cash payments that dwindle in size over a short time), which resemble cash property settlements, Congress added §71(f), which recaptures an amount in the third post separation year (i.e., the payor has gross income and the payee has a deduction). The recapture occurs in the third year of post-separation payments, but it arises by reference to an analysis of first and second year post-separation payments.

Notes

Moving Expenses
8.5

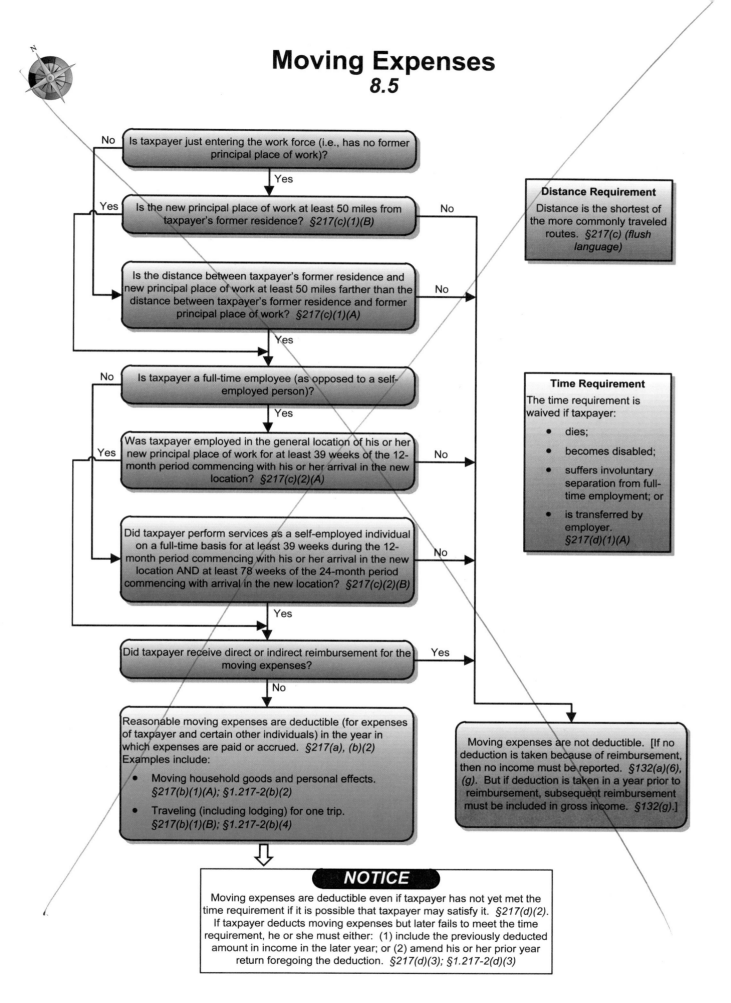

Is taxpayer just entering the work force (i.e., has no former principal place of work)?

No → **Yes** ↓

Is the new principal place of work at least 50 miles from taxpayer's former residence? *§217(c)(1)(B)*

Yes ↓ — **No** →

Is the distance between taxpayer's former residence and new principal place of work at least 50 miles farther than the distance between taxpayer's former residence and former principal place of work? *§217(c)(1)(A)*

No →   **Yes** ↓

Is taxpayer a full-time employee (as opposed to a self-employed person)?

No → **Yes** ↓

Was taxpayer employed in the general location of his or her new principal place of work for at least 39 weeks of the 12-month period commencing with his or her arrival in the new location? *§217(c)(2)(A)*

Yes ↓ — **No** →

Did taxpayer perform services as a self-employed individual on a full-time basis for at least 39 weeks during the 12-month period commencing with his or her arrival in the new location AND at least 78 weeks of the 24-month period commencing with arrival in the new location? *§217(c)(2)(B)*

No →   **Yes** ↓

Did taxpayer receive direct or indirect reimbursement for the moving expenses?

Yes →   **No** ↓

Reasonable moving expenses are deductible (for expenses of taxpayer and certain other individuals) in the year in which expenses are paid or accrued. *§217(a), (b)(2)*
Examples include:

- Moving household goods and personal effects. *§217(b)(1)(A); §1.217-2(b)(2)*
- Traveling (including lodging) for one trip. *§217(b)(1)(B); §1.217-2(b)(4)*

Distance Requirement

Distance is the shortest of the more commonly traveled routes. *§217(c) (flush language)*

Time Requirement

The time requirement is waived if taxpayer:

- dies;
- becomes disabled;
- suffers involuntary separation from full-time employment; or
- is transferred by employer. *§217(d)(1)(A)*

79

Moving expenses are not deductible. [If no deduction is taken because of reimbursement, then no income must be reported. *§132(a)(6), (g)*. But if deduction is taken in a year prior to reimbursement, subsequent reimbursement must be included in gross income. *§132(g)*.]

NOTICE

Moving expenses are deductible even if taxpayer has not yet met the time requirement if it is possible that taxpayer may satisfy it. *§217(d)(2)*. If taxpayer deducts moving expenses but later fails to meet the time requirement, he or she must either: (1) include the previously deducted amount in income in the later year; or (2) amend his or her prior year return foregoing the deduction. *§217(d)(3); §1.217-2(d)(3)*

Notes

Hobby Losses
9.0

(handwritten: Disallowed thru 2025)

(handwritten top right: Y)

Is taxpayer an individual, S corporation, estate, or trust? *§1.183-1(a)* → **No**

↓ **Yes**

Was the activity profitable (i.e., gross income exceeded deductions) for three or more years in the five-year period ending with the year in question? *§183(d) (also providing a different rule for horse breeding activities)* → **Yes**

↓ **No**

Is the activity engaged in for profit? §183(c) incorporates standards applied by §§162 & 212. §1.183-2(b) provides the following factors that should be taken into account:

(1) The manner in which taxpayer carries on the activity;
(2) The expertise of taxpayer or his or her advisors;
(3) The time and effort expended by taxpayer in carrying on the activity;
(4) The expectation that assets used in the activity may appreciate in value;
(5) The success of taxpayer in carrying on other similar or dissimilar activities;
(6) The taxpayer's history of income or losses with respect to the activity;
(7) The amount of occasional profits, if any, which are earned;
(8) The financial status of taxpayer; and
(9) Elements of personal pleasure or recreation.

(handwritten: Biz activity v. hobby)

No ←   → **Yes**

81

Activity Not Engaged in for Profit
Deductions attributable to the hobby activity are allowed only to the extent of hobby income. *§183(b)*. Regulations create the following three tiers of permitted deductions:

↓

Tier 1
Deductions that would be allowable whether or not the activity is engaged in for profit (e.g., state and local property taxes under §164). *§1.183-1(b)(1)*. ALLOWED in full, subject to any limitations to which they would otherwise be subject.

(handwritten: only deductions allowed (itemized right now))

↓

Tier 2
Deductions that would be allowable if the activity had been conducted for profit but that do not result in basis adjustments (e.g., business expenses under §162). *§1.183-1(b)(2)*. ALLOWED only to the extent that gross income from the activity exceeds Tier 1 deductions.

↓

Tier 3
Deductions that would be allowable if the activity had been conducted for profit but that result in basis adjustments (e.g., depreciation). *§1.183-1(b)(3)*. ALLOWED only to the extent that gross income from the activity exceeds Tier 1 and Tier 2 deductions.

Activity Engaged in for Profit
Is the activity a "trade or business" activity or an "investment" activity?

Trade or Business ←   → **Investment**

Expenses
§162. See Maps 7.0-7.2

Expenses
§212. See Map 7.4

↓   ↓

Losses
§165(c)(1). See Map 7.3

Losses
§165(c)(2). See Map 7.4

(handwritten: misc + not currently deductible)

↓   ↓

Depreciation
§167(a)(1)
See Maps 7.6-7.7

Depreciation
§167(a)(2)
See Maps 7.6-7.7

Notes

The At Risk Rules
9.1

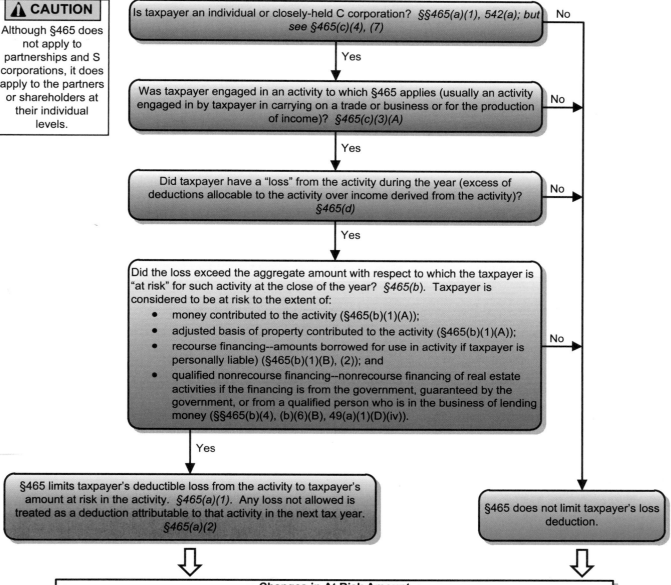

⚠ CAUTION

Although §465 does not apply to partnerships and S corporations, it does apply to the partners or shareholders at their individual levels.

Is taxpayer an individual or closely-held C corporation? *§§465(a)(1), 542(a); but see §465(c)(4), (7)* — **No**

↓ **Yes**

Was taxpayer engaged in an activity to which §465 applies (usually an activity engaged in by taxpayer in carrying on a trade or business or for the production of income)? *§465(c)(3)(A)* — **No**

↓ **Yes**

Did taxpayer have a "loss" from the activity during the year (excess of deductions allocable to the activity over income derived from the activity)? *§465(d)* — **No**

↓ **Yes**

Did the loss exceed the aggregate amount with respect to which the taxpayer is "at risk" for such activity at the close of the year? *§465(b)*. Taxpayer is considered to be at risk to the extent of:
- money contributed to the activity (§465(b)(1)(A));
- adjusted basis of property contributed to the activity (§465(b)(1)(A));
- recourse financing--amounts borrowed for use in activity if taxpayer is personally liable) (§465(b)(1)(B), (2)); and
- qualified nonrecourse financing--nonrecourse financing of real estate activities if the financing is from the government, guaranteed by the government, or from a qualified person who is in the business of lending money (§§465(b)(4), (b)(6)(B), 49(a)(1)(D)(iv)).

— **No**

↓ **Yes**

§465 limits taxpayer's deductible loss from the activity to taxpayer's amount at risk in the activity. *§465(a)(1)*. Any loss not allowed is treated as a deduction attributable to that activity in the next tax year. *§465(a)(2)*

§465 does not limit taxpayer's loss deduction.

83

Changes in At Risk Amount

Taxpayer's at risk amount is calculated each year, taking into account events during the year.
At risk amount *increases* if:
- The activity generates income
- Taxpayer contributes additional money or property
- Taxpayer incurs additional recourse debt or qualified nonrecourse debt

At risk amount *decreases* if:
- The at risk rules permit a loss to be deducted (amount deducted reduces at risk) *§465(b)(5)*
- Taxpayer withdraws money from the activity

Recapture of Losses Where At Risk Amount is Less than Zero

If some event would cause at risk amount to go below zero (e.g., distribution to taxpayer or conversion of qualified debt to nonqualified debt), the Code requires taxpayer to take an amount into income sufficient to produce a zero at risk amount. Taxpayer is permitted a corresponding loss carryover equal to the amount of that income that is recaptured. *§465(e)*

Notes

84

The Passive Loss Rules
9.2

Y

Definition of Activity

Identifying an "activity" is important because how undertakings are combined or separated may produce different tax results. The regulations look for the "appropriate economic unit." *§1.469-4(c)(1)*

Is taxpayer an individual, estate, trust, closely-held C corporation, or personal service corporation? *§§469(a)(2), (j)(1), 465(a)(1)(B), 542(a)(2)*

No →

Yes ↓

Was taxpayer engaged in any *passive activities*?

- A passive activity is a business or profit-seeking activity in which taxpayer *does not materially participate* (i.e., is not involved on a regular, continuous, and substantial basis in the operations of the activity). *§469(c)(1), (6), (h)(1)*
- The regulations provide a *set of bright line tests* to determine whether the material participation test is satisfied. *§1.469-5T*
- A *limited partnership interest* is generally deemed passive, regardless of level of actual participation. *§469(h)(2); but see §1.469-5T(e)(2)*
- A *rental activity* is generally passive, even if taxpayer materially participates in the activity. *§469(c)(2), (j)(8); but see §469(c)(7)(A) & (B) (rental real property trades), §469(i) (mom & pop rental real estate activities)*

(1) 500 (H)/hr/yr
(2) similar to others
(3) material participant

No →

Yes ↓

85

Did taxpayer's losses from all passive activities exceed income from such activities during the year?

No →

Yes ↓

Dispositions of Passive Activities

Dispositions of passive activities can release some or all of the previously suspended losses. *§469(g)*

The excess (net loss from all of taxpayer's passive activities for the year) is disallowed this year, and cannot be deducted against non-passive income. *§469(a)*. It carries over as a deduction for the next year where it can be used to offset passive income. *§469(b), (d)(1)*

§469 does not apply.

Small Rental Real Estate Activities

A special rule provides that up to $25,000 of losses attributable to rental real estate activities can be offset against non-passive income if taxpayer: (1) *actively participates* in the rental activity (not as stringent as material participation rule); and (2) is at least a *10% owner*. *§469(i); but see §469(i)(6)(C) (limited partner cannot actively participate)*. But the $25,000 amount is reduced by $1 for every $2 by which taxpayer's adjusted gross income (determined without regard to passive losses) exceeds $100,000. *§469(i)(3)(A)*

Notes

Home Office Deductions
9.3

Y

87

NOTICE

Use by family and friends without paying fair rental is deemed personal use of the residence by taxpayer. *§280(d)(2)*

Did taxpayer use a *dwelling unit* (e.g., house, apartment, condo) during the year as a *residence* (dwelling unit used for personal purposes for greater of 14 days or 10% of days rented during the year)? *§280A(d)(1), (f)(1)*

→ **No** → Go to Map 9.0

↓ **Yes**

Was a portion of the home used *exclusively* and *regularly* as the *principal place of business* (PPOB) for any trade or business of the taxpayer? *§280A(c)(1)(A)*

- §280A(c)(1) (last sentence): PPOB test met if home office used for administrative or management activities of any trade or business and if there is no other fixed location for conducting such activities.
- *Comm'r v. Soliman*: The two primary factors in determining whether home office is PPOB: (1) relative importance of activities performed at each business location; and (2) amount of time spent at each location.

} If N/A

← **Yes**

↓ **No**

Was a portion of the home used *exclusively* and *regularly* as a place of business, used by patients, clients, or customers in meeting/dealing with taxpayer in his trade or business? *§280A(c)(1)(B)*

← **Yes**

↓ **No**

Was a separate structure, which is not attached to the dwelling unit, used *exclusively* and *regularly* in connection with taxpayer's trade or business? *§280A(c)(1)(C)*

← **Yes**   **No** →

↓

Is taxpayer an *employee*?

No ←   ↓ **Yes**

Was the exclusive use by taxpayer for the *convenience of his or her employer*? *§280A(c) (flush language)*

← **Yes**   **No** →

↓

- Certain expenses (e.g., real estate taxes, mortgage interest,) are *fully deductible* without respect to the home office. *§280A(b)*
- Other expenses (e.g., insurance, utilities, depreciation) are *partially deductible* based on percentage of home used for business, subject to the following income limitation:

  | Gross income from business |
  | Business expenses not related to home office |
  | Portion of taxes & interest allocable to home office |
  | Limit on deduction of insurance, utilities, & depreciation (ordering rules require depreciation to be taken last) |

  §280A(c)(5); Prop. Treas. Reg. §1.280A-2(i)(5), -2(i)(7). Disallowed amounts carry forward. *§280A(c)(5) (flush language)*

- Some expenses (e.g, lawn care) are not deductible.

- Certain expenses (e.g., real estate taxes, mortgage interest) are fully deductible without regard to use of the home as a business. *§280A(b)*
- Other expenses (e.g., insurance, utilities, depreciation) are not deductible. *§280A(a)*

Notes

88

Vacation Home Deductions
9.4

Y

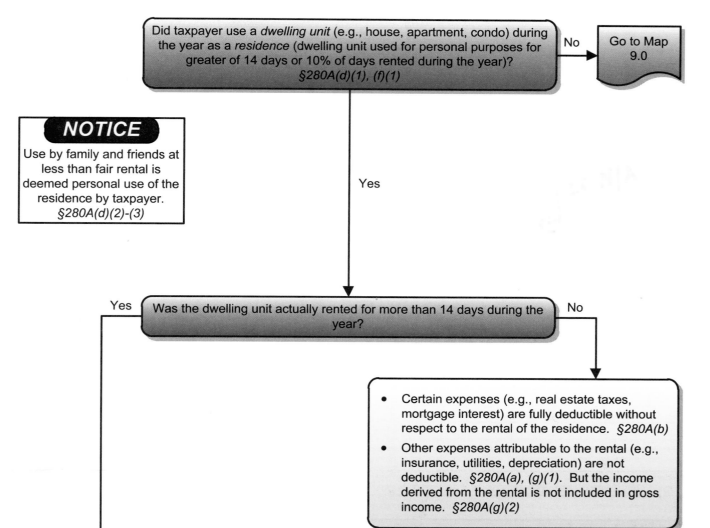

Did taxpayer use a *dwelling unit* (e.g., house, apartment, condo) during the year as a *residence* (dwelling unit used for personal purposes for greater of 14 days or 10% of days rented during the year)? §280A(d)(1), (f)(1)

No → Go to Map 9.0

Go to Map 9.0

NOTICE
Use by family and friends at less than fair rental is deemed personal use of the residence by taxpayer. §280A(d)(2)-(3)

Yes

Was the dwelling unit actually rented for more than 14 days during the year?

Yes / No

No branch:
- Certain expenses (e.g., real estate taxes, mortgage interest) are fully deductible without respect to the rental of the residence. §280A(b)
- Other expenses attributable to the rental (e.g., insurance, utilities, depreciation) are not deductible. §280A(a), (g)(1). But the income derived from the rental is not included in gross income. §280A(g)(2)

89

Yes branch:
- Certain expenses (e.g., real estate taxes, mortgage interest) are *fully deductible* without respect to the rental of the residence. §280A(b)
- Other expenses (e.g., insurance, utilities, depreciation) are *partially deductible* based on days when unit is rented (i.e., days of rental divided by days of use), subject to the following income cap:

  _ Gross income derived from rental
  _ Rental expenses (e.g., advertising & management fees)
  Taxes & interest allocable to days when unit is rented*
  _____
  Limit on deduction of insurance, utilities, & depreciation (ordering rules require depreciation to be taken last)

§280A(c)(3), (5), (e)(1); Prop. Treas. Reg. §1.280A-3(c)(2)-(3). Disallowed amounts carry forward. §280A(c)(5) (flush language)

*NOTE: Taxes & interest allocable to rental use is based on days of rental divided by *days of use*. Prop. Treas. Reg. §1.280A-3(d)(1) & (3). Some courts have used days of rental divided by *total days in the year*.

Notes

90

Losses Between Related Parties
9.5

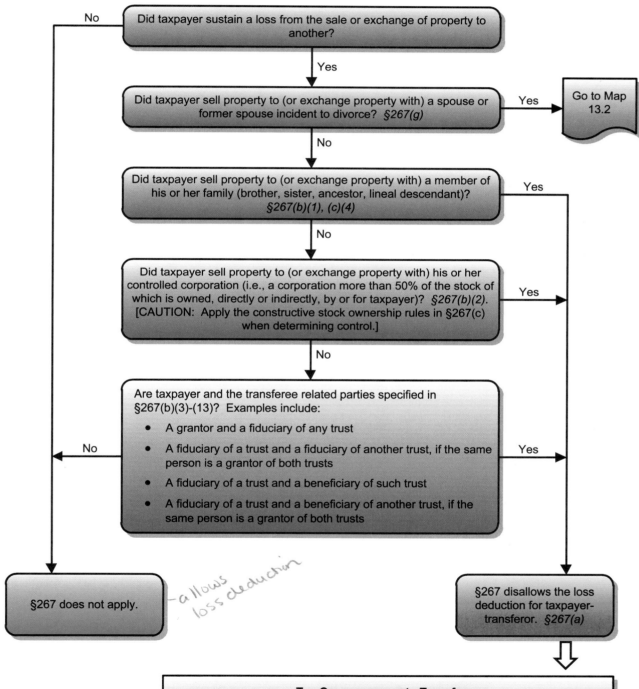

⚠ WARNING
You should not begin with this map. You should be directed here from Map 3.0.

No ← Did taxpayer sustain a loss from the sale or exchange of property to another?

↓ **Yes**

Did taxpayer sell property to (or exchange property with) a spouse or former spouse incident to divorce? *§267(g)* → **Yes** → Go to Map 13.2

↓ **No**

Did taxpayer sell property to (or exchange property with) a member of his or her family (brother, sister, ancestor, lineal descendant)? *§267(b)(1), (c)(4)* → **Yes**

↓ **No**

Did taxpayer sell property to (or exchange property with) his or her controlled corporation (i.e., a corporation more than 50% of the stock of which is owned, directly or indirectly, by or for taxpayer)? *§267(b)(2)*. [CAUTION: Apply the constructive stock ownership rules in §267(c) when determining control.] → **Yes**

↓ **No**

Are taxpayer and the transferee related parties specified in §267(b)(3)-(13)? Examples include:

- A grantor and a fiduciary of any trust
- A fiduciary of a trust and a fiduciary of another trust, if the same person is a grantor of both trusts
- A fiduciary of a trust and a beneficiary of such trust
- A fiduciary of a trust and a beneficiary of another trust, if the same person is a grantor of both trusts

No ← → **Yes**

§267 does not apply. — *allows loss deduction*

§267 disallows the loss deduction for taxpayer-transferor. *§267(a)*

↓

Tax Consequences to Transferee
If the transferee later sells or otherwise disposes of the property at a gain, the gain shall be recognized only to the extent that it exceeds the loss that was previously disallowed to the transferor. *§267(d) (giving transferee the benefit of the transferor's loss but only to a limited extent)*

Notes

Losses from Wash Sales of Stock
9.6

> **⚠ WARNING**
> You should not begin with this map. You should be directed here from Map 3.0.

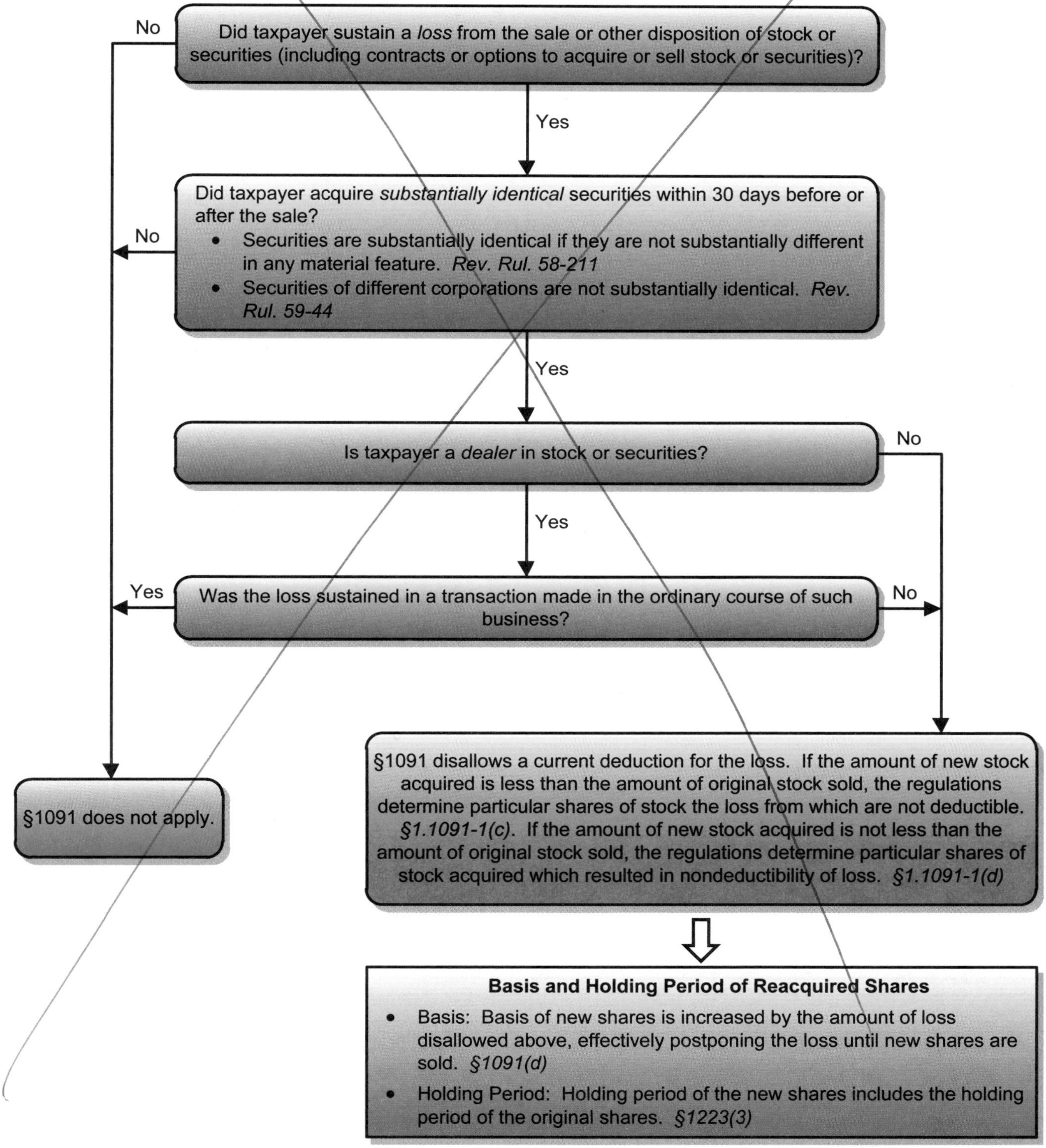

No ← Did taxpayer sustain a *loss* from the sale or other disposition of stock or securities (including contracts or options to acquire or sell stock or securities)?

Yes ↓

Did taxpayer acquire *substantially identical* securities within 30 days before or after the sale?
- Securities are substantially identical if they are not substantially different in any material feature. *Rev. Rul. 58-211*
- Securities of different corporations are not substantially identical. *Rev. Rul. 59-44*

No ←

Yes ↓

Is taxpayer a *dealer* in stock or securities? **No** →

Yes ↓

Yes ← Was the loss sustained in a transaction made in the ordinary course of such business? **No** →

§1091 does not apply.

§1091 disallows a current deduction for the loss. If the amount of new stock acquired is less than the amount of original stock sold, the regulations determine particular shares of stock the loss from which are not deductible. *§1.1091-1(c)*. If the amount of new stock acquired is not less than the amount of original stock sold, the regulations determine particular shares of stock acquired which resulted in nondeductibility of loss. *§1.1091-1(d)*

⇩

Basis and Holding Period of Reacquired Shares
- Basis: Basis of new shares is increased by the amount of loss disallowed above, effectively postponing the loss until new shares are sold. *§1091(d)*
- Holding Period: Holding period of the new shares includes the holding period of the original shares. *§1223(3)*

Notes

94

Getting to Adjusted Gross Income and Taxable Income
10.0

Premise

The Code establishes a hierarchy for authorized deductions. *§§62, 63.* Some deductions are taken from gross income in arriving at adjusted gross income. Other deductions are taken from adjusted gross income in arriving at taxable income. This Map considers where in the tax calculation deductions are taken, and the significance of the deduction hierarchy.

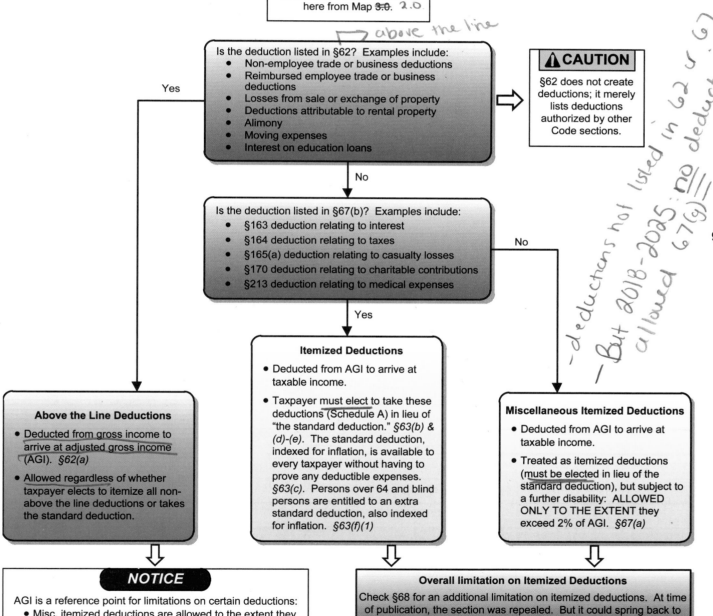

⚠ WARNING

You should not begin with this map. You should be directed here from Map ~~3.0~~. 2.0

[handwritten] → above the line

⚠ CAUTION

§62 does not create deductions; it merely lists deductions authorized by other Code sections.

Is the deduction listed in §62? Examples include:
- Non-employee trade or business deductions
- Reimbursed employee trade or business deductions
- Losses from sale or exchange of property
- Deductions attributable to rental property
- Alimony
- Moving expenses
- Interest on education loans

Yes / *No*

Is the deduction listed in §67(b)? Examples include:
- §163 deduction relating to interest
- §164 deduction relating to taxes
- §165(a) deduction relating to casualty losses
- §170 deduction relating to charitable contributions
- §213 deduction relating to medical expenses

No / *Yes*

95

[handwritten margin] — deductions not listed in 62 & .67 = no deduction — But 2018-2025 allowed 67(g)

Above the Line Deductions
- Deducted from gross income to arrive at adjusted gross income (AGI). *§62(a)*
- Allowed regardless of whether taxpayer elects to itemize all non-above the line deductions or takes the standard deduction.

Itemized Deductions
- Deducted from AGI to arrive at taxable income.
- Taxpayer must elect to take these deductions (Schedule A) in lieu of "the standard deduction." *§63(b) & (d)-(e).* The standard deduction, indexed for inflation, is available to every taxpayer without having to prove any deductible expenses. *§63(c).* Persons over 64 and blind persons are entitled to an extra standard deduction, also indexed for inflation. *§63(f)(1)*

Miscellaneous Itemized Deductions
- Deducted from AGI to arrive at taxable income.
- Treated as itemized deductions (must be elected in lieu of the standard deduction), but subject to a further disability: ALLOWED ONLY TO THE EXTENT they exceed 2% of AGI. *§67(a)*

NOTICE

AGI is a reference point for limitations on certain deductions:
- Misc. itemized deductions are allowed to the extent they exceed 2% of AGI.
- Medical expenses are deductible to the extent they exceed 7.5% of AGI.
- Net casualty losses are deductible to the extent they exceed 10% of AGI.
- Most charitable contributions are limited to 50% of AGI.

Overall limitation on Itemized Deductions

Check §68 for an additional limitation on itemized deductions. At time of publication, the section was repealed. But it could spring back to life.

[handwritten at bottom]
Gross Income
- Above the Line
Adj. GI
- Standard or Itemized Deduction
- Personal + Dependency

[handwritten right margin, vertical] A Deduction = Taxable Income

[handwritten top right] Y

Notes

Personal and Dependency Exemptions
10.1

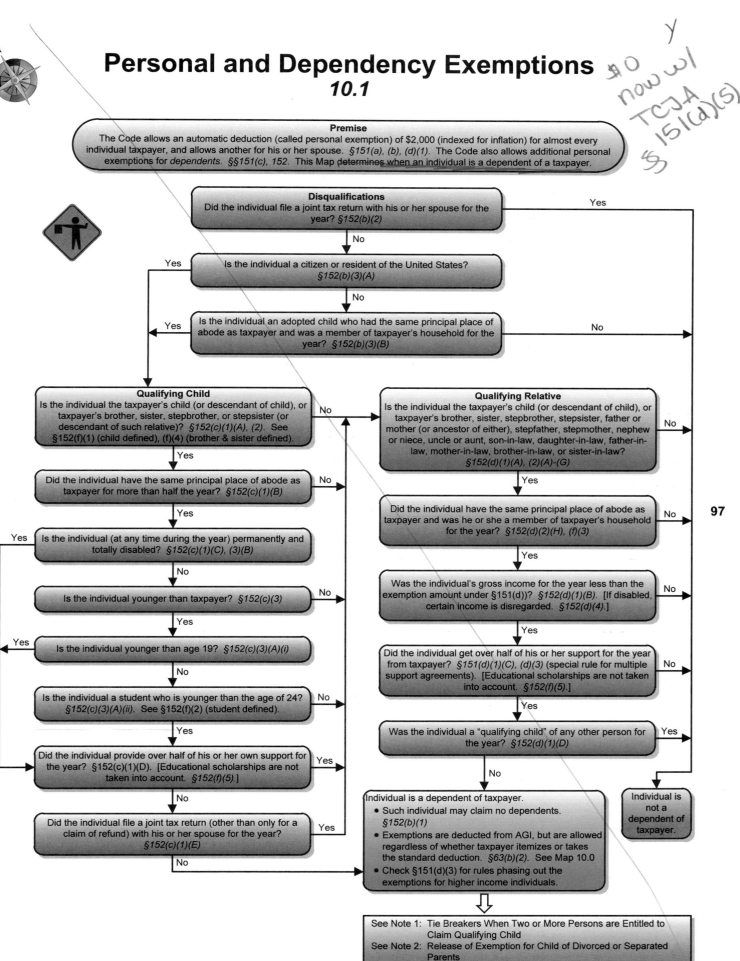

(handwritten top right: Y / $0 now w/ TCJA / §151(d)(5))

Premise
The Code allows an automatic deduction (called personal exemption) of $2,000 (indexed for inflation) for almost every individual taxpayer, and allows another for his or her spouse. *§151(a), (b), (d)(1)*. The Code also allows additional personal exemptions for *dependents*. *§§151(c), 152*. This Map determines when an individual is a dependent of a taxpayer.

Disqualifications
Did the individual file a joint tax return with his or her spouse for the year? *§152(b)(2)* — Yes

No

Is the individual a citizen or resident of the United States? *§152(b)(3)(A)* — Yes

No

Is the individual an adopted child who had the same principal place of abode as taxpayer and was a member of taxpayer's household for the year? *§152(b)(3)(B)* — Yes / No

Qualifying Child
Is the individual the taxpayer's child (or descendant of child), or taxpayer's brother, sister, stepbrother, or stepsister (or descendant of such relative)? *§152(c)(1)(A), (2)*. See §152(f)(1) (child defined), (f)(4) (brother & sister defined). — No →

Yes

Did the individual have the same principal place of abode as taxpayer for more than half the year? *§152(c)(1)(B)* — No →

Yes

Is the individual (at any time during the year) permanently and totally disabled? *§152(c)(1)(C), (3)(B)* — Yes →

No

Is the individual younger than taxpayer? *§152(c)(3)* — No →

Yes

Is the individual younger than age 19? *§152(c)(3)(A)(i)* — Yes →

No

Is the individual a student who is younger than the age of 24? *§152(c)(3)(A)(ii)*. See §152(f)(2) (student defined). — No →

Yes

Did the individual provide over half of his or her own support for the year? §152(c)(1)(D). [Educational scholarships are not taken into account. *§152(f)(5)*.] — Yes →

No

Did the individual file a joint tax return (other than only for a claim of refund) with his or her spouse for the year? *§152(c)(1)(E)* — Yes →

No

Qualifying Relative
Is the individual the taxpayer's child (or descendant of child), or taxpayer's brother, sister, stepbrother, stepsister, father or mother (or ancestor of either), stepfather, stepmother, nephew or niece, uncle or aunt, son-in-law, daughter-in-law, father-in-law, mother-in-law, brother-in-law, or sister-in-law? *§152(d)(1)(A), (2)(A)-(G)* — No →

Yes

Did the individual have the same principal place of abode as taxpayer and was he or she a member of taxpayer's household for the year? *§152(d)(2)(H), (f)(3)* — No →

97

Yes

Was the individual's gross income for the year less than the exemption amount under §151(d))? *§152(d)(1)(B)*. [If disabled, certain income is disregarded. *§152(d)(4)*.] — No →

Yes

Did the individual get over half of his or her support for the year from taxpayer? *§151(d)(1)(C), (d)(3)* (special rule for multiple support agreements). [Educational scholarships are not taken into account. *§152(f)(5)*.] — No →

Yes

Was the individual a "qualifying child" of any other person for the year? *§152(d)(1)(D)* — Yes →

No

Individual is a dependent of taxpayer.
- Such individual may claim no dependents. *§152(b)(1)*
- Exemptions are deducted from AGI, but are allowed regardless of whether taxpayer itemizes or takes the standard deduction. *§63(b)(2)*. See Map 10.0
- Check §151(d)(3) for rules phasing out the exemptions for higher income individuals.

Individual is not a dependent of taxpayer.

See Note 1: Tie Breakers When Two or More Persons are Entitled to Claim Qualifying Child
See Note 2: Release of Exemption for Child of Divorced or Separated Parents

Notes

Personal and Dependency Exemptions
10.1 Notes

Y

Note 1

Tie Breaker When Two or More Persons are Entitled to Claim an Individual as a Qualifying Child

When two or more persons are entitled to claim an individual as a *qualifying child*, the following tie breaking rules apply:

1. If one person is a parent: Parent gets the dependency exemption. *§152(c)(4)(A)(i)*

2. If neither person is a parent: Person with the highest adjusted gross income gets the dependency exemption. *§152(c)(4)(A)(ii)*

3. If both persons are parents: Parent with whom child resided for the longer period of time during the year (custodial parent) gets the dependency exemption. *§152(c)(4)(B)(i)*. If child resides with both parents for the same amount of time during the year, Parent with the highest adjusted gross income gets the dependency exemption. *§152(c)(4)(B)(ii)*. But see Note 2, below.

Note 2

Release of Claim to Exemption for Child of Divorced or Separated Parents (*§152(e)*)

1. If a child receives over half of his or her support during the year from his or her parents who are divorced or legally separated (or who are separated under a written separation agreement or who live apart during the last six months of the year),

   AND

2. If such child is in custody of one or both of the parents for more than half of the year,

   THEN

3. The custodial parent (parent who has custody of child for the greater portion of the year and who is generally entitled to the dependency exemption), can transfer the dependency exemption to the non-custodial parent,

   IF

4. The custodial parent signs a waiver that he or she will not claim the child as a dependent and attaches the waiver to his or her tax return.

99

Notes

The Cash Method
11.0

handwritten: expenditure that benefits more than 1 period

Premise

This Map considers the cash method of accounting, which is the method that most individuals employ in determining the proper timing of income and deductions. The other main method of accounting, the accrual method, is considered in Map 11.1.

⚠ CAUTION

These timing rules do not establish that an item is income or that one has the right to deduct an expense. They just tell us when to report or deduct it.

Deductions Under the Cash Method

Was the medium of payment an instrument (such as a check), as opposed to cash, property, or services? — **No** →

Yes ↓

Was the check honored and paid in due course with no restrictions as to the time and manner of payment? — **No** →

Yes ↓

Did taxpayer prepay an otherwise deductible expense in a year earlier than the year to which the expense relates (e.g. prepaid rent, interest, and other expenses that benefit more than one year)? — **Yes** →

No ↓

Is there is special rule that permits a current deduction (e.g., §461(g)(2) (points), §1.263(a)-4(f) (12-month rule))? — **No** → Payment must be capitalized and may be deductible in later years through depreciation or amorization.

Yes → Deduction is allowed upon actual payment. There is no doctrine of constructive payment

Mailing/transfer of the check does not set the year of deduction.

NOTICE

Checks are generally considered cash equivalents. An evidence of obligation (such as an IOU note) is not a cash equivalent if there is a substantial risk of non-payment and no third party is likely to be willing to buy the obligation for close to fair value.

Income Under the Cash Method

Was the income from the sale or other disposition of property on a deferred payment basis? — **Yes** → Go to Map 11.2

No ↓

Was the income received in the form of an instrument (such as a check), as opposed to cash, property, or services? — **Yes** →

No ↓

Was the instrument a cash equivalent, i.e., readily negotiable at or near its face value? — **Yes** →

No ↓

Prior to actual receipt, was the income credited to taxpayer's account, set apart for him, or otherwise made available so that he may draw upon it at any time? — **Yes** →

No ↓

Was taxpayer's control of its receipt subject to substantial limitations or restrictions? — **No** → Taxpayer has income when item is *actually* received.

Yes ↓

Taxpayer has income when item is *constructively* received

In the case of a cash equivalent evidence of obligation, the present value of the obligation is the amount of current income.

Taxpayer does not have income upon receipt of the instrument or obligation.

Tax Benefit Rule

If taxpayer properly takes a deduction in one year and recovers the amount deducted in a later year, the taxpayer usually must take the amount of the recovery into income. *Bliss Dairy, Inc. v. U.S.; §111*

Claim of Right Doctrine

Earnings held under an unrestricted claim of right must be reported as income when actually or constructively received even if another person is asserting a claim to those same funds. If obliged to refund the amounts, a deduction in year of repayment is allowable. *North American Oil Consolidated v. Burnet; §341*

Notes

102

The Accrual Method
11.1

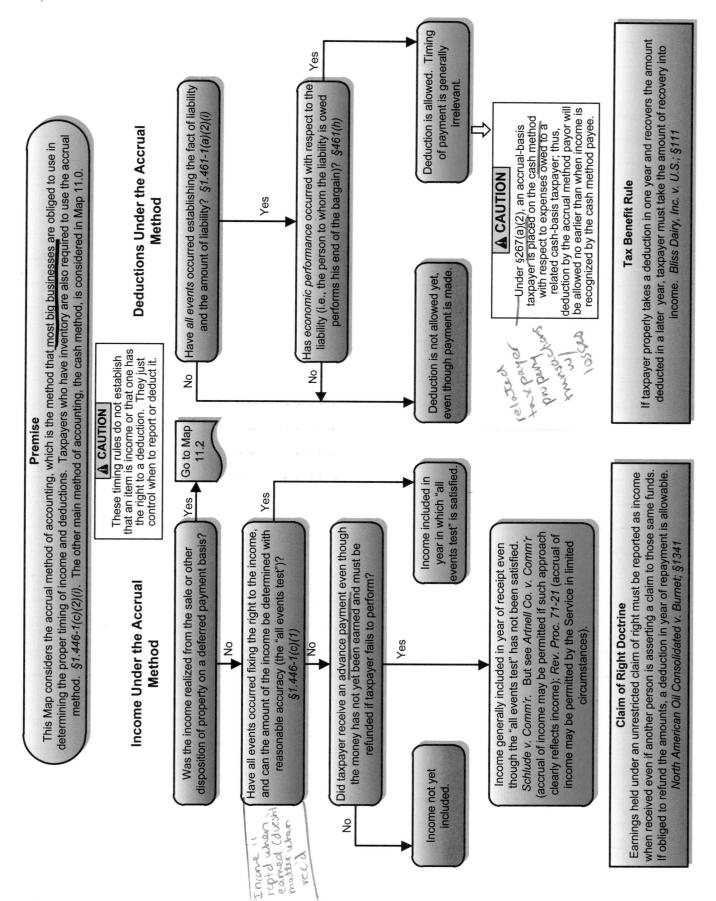

Premise

This Map considers the accrual method of accounting, which is the method that most big businesses are obliged to use in determining the proper timing of income and deductions. Taxpayers who have inventory are also required to use the accrual method. *§1.446-1(c)(2)(i)*. The other main method of accounting, the cash method, is considered in Map 11.0.

⚠ CAUTION

These timing rules do not establish that an item is income or that one has the right to a deduction. They just control when to report or deduct it.

Deductions Under the Accrual Method

Have *all events* occurred establishing the fact of liability and the amount of liability? *§1.461-1(a)(2)(i)*

No → Yes →

Has *economic performance* occurred with respect to the liability (i.e., the person to whom the liability is owed performs his end of the bargain)? *§461(h)*

Yes → Deduction is allowed. Timing of payment is generally irrelevant.

No → Deduction is not allowed yet, even though payment is made.

⚠ CAUTION

Under §267(a)(2), an accrual-basis taxpayer is placed on the cash method with respect to expenses owed to a related cash-basis taxpayer; thus, deduction by the accrual method payor will be allowed no earlier than when income is recognized by the cash method payee.

Tax Benefit Rule

If taxpayer properly takes a deduction in one year and recovers the amount deducted in a later year, taxpayer must take the amount of recovery into income. *Bliss Dairy, Inc. v. U.S.; §111*

Income Under the Accrual Method

Was the income realized from the sale or other disposition of property on a deferred payment basis?

Yes → Go to Map 11.2

No →

Have all events occurred fixing the right to the income, and can the amount of the income be determined with reasonable accuracy (the "all events test")? *§1.446-1(c)(1)*

No → Yes → Income included in year in which "all events test" is satisfied.

Did taxpayer receive an advance payment even though the money has not yet been earned and must be refunded if taxpayer fails to perform?

No → Income not yet included.

Yes → Income generally included in year of receipt even though the "all events test" has not been satisfied. *Schlude v. Comm'r.* But see *Artnell Co. v. Comm'r.* (accrual of income may be permitted if such approach clearly reflects income); *Rev. Proc. 71-21* (accrual of income may be permitted by the Service in limited circumstances).

Claim of Right Doctrine

Earnings held under an unrestricted claim of right must be reported as income when received even if another person is asserting a claim to those same funds. If obliged to refund the amounts, a deduction in year of repayment is allowable. *North American Oil Consolidated v. Burnet; §1341*

Notes

Installment Sales
11.2

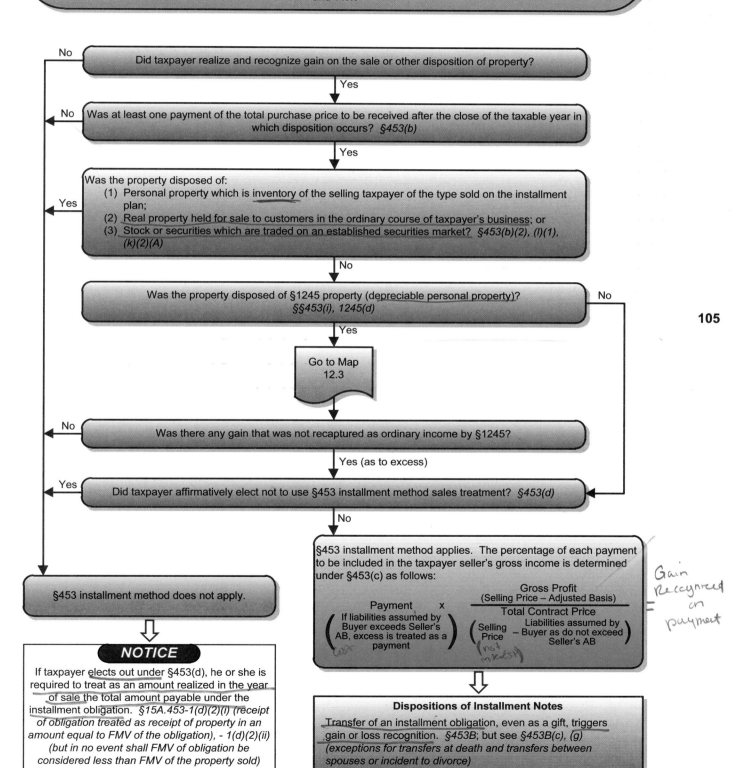

Premise

This Map considers §453, which permits "installment method" reporting of gain on an "installment sale" of property (i.e., seller can recognize tax gain over time as payments are received as opposed to recognizing tax gain in full in the year of sale. The installment method is an exception to both the cash and accrual methods of accounting, which are covered by Maps 11.0 and 11.1.

No ← Did taxpayer realize and recognize gain on the sale or other disposition of property?

Yes ↓

No ← Was at least one payment of the total purchase price to be received after the close of the taxable year in which disposition occurs? *§453(b)*

Yes ↓

Yes ← Was the property disposed of:
(1) Personal property which is inventory of the selling taxpayer of the type sold on the installment plan;
(2) Real property held for sale to customers in the ordinary course of taxpayer's business; or
(3) Stock or securities which are traded on an established securities market? *§453(b)(2), (l)(1), (k)(2)(A)*

No ↓

Was the property disposed of §1245 property (depreciable personal property)? *§§453(i), 1245(d)* → No

105

Yes ↓

Go to Map 12.3

No ← Was there any gain that was not recaptured as ordinary income by §1245?

Yes (as to excess) ↓

Yes ← Did taxpayer affirmatively elect not to use §453 installment method sales treatment? *§453(d)* ←

No ↓

§453 installment method does not apply.

§453 installment method applies. The percentage of each payment to be included in the taxpayer seller's gross income is determined under §453(c) as follows:

$$\text{Payment} \begin{pmatrix} \text{If liabilities assumed by} \\ \text{Buyer exceeds Seller's} \\ \text{AB, excess is treated as a} \\ \text{payment} \end{pmatrix} \times \frac{\text{Gross Profit}}{\text{Total Contract Price}} \begin{pmatrix} \text{Selling} \\ \text{Price} \end{pmatrix} \begin{pmatrix} \text{Liabilities assumed by} \\ \text{Buyer as do not exceed} \\ \text{Seller's AB} \end{pmatrix}$$

Gain Recognized on payment

NOTICE

If taxpayer elects out under §453(d), he or she is required to treat as an amount realized in the year of sale the total amount payable under the installment obligation. *§15A.453-1(d)(2)(I) (receipt of obligation treated as receipt of property in an amount equal to FMV of the obligation), - 1(d)(2)(ii) (but in no event shall FMV of obligation be considered less than FMV of the property sold)*

Dispositions of Installment Notes

Transfer of an installment obligation, even as a gift, triggers gain or loss recognition. *§453B; but see §453B(c), (g) (exceptions for transfers at death and transfers between spouses or incident to divorce)*

Notes

Capital Gains and Losses
Overview
12.0

Premise

Maps 3.0, 7.3, 7.4, and 8.1 considered gains and losses from property transactions. After determining whether gain is included in gross income or whether loss is deductible from gross income, the "character" of the gain or loss must be determined. A recognized gain or deductible loss is characterized as either *capital* or *ordinary*.

⚠ **WARNING**

You should not begin with this map. You should be directed here from Map 3.0.

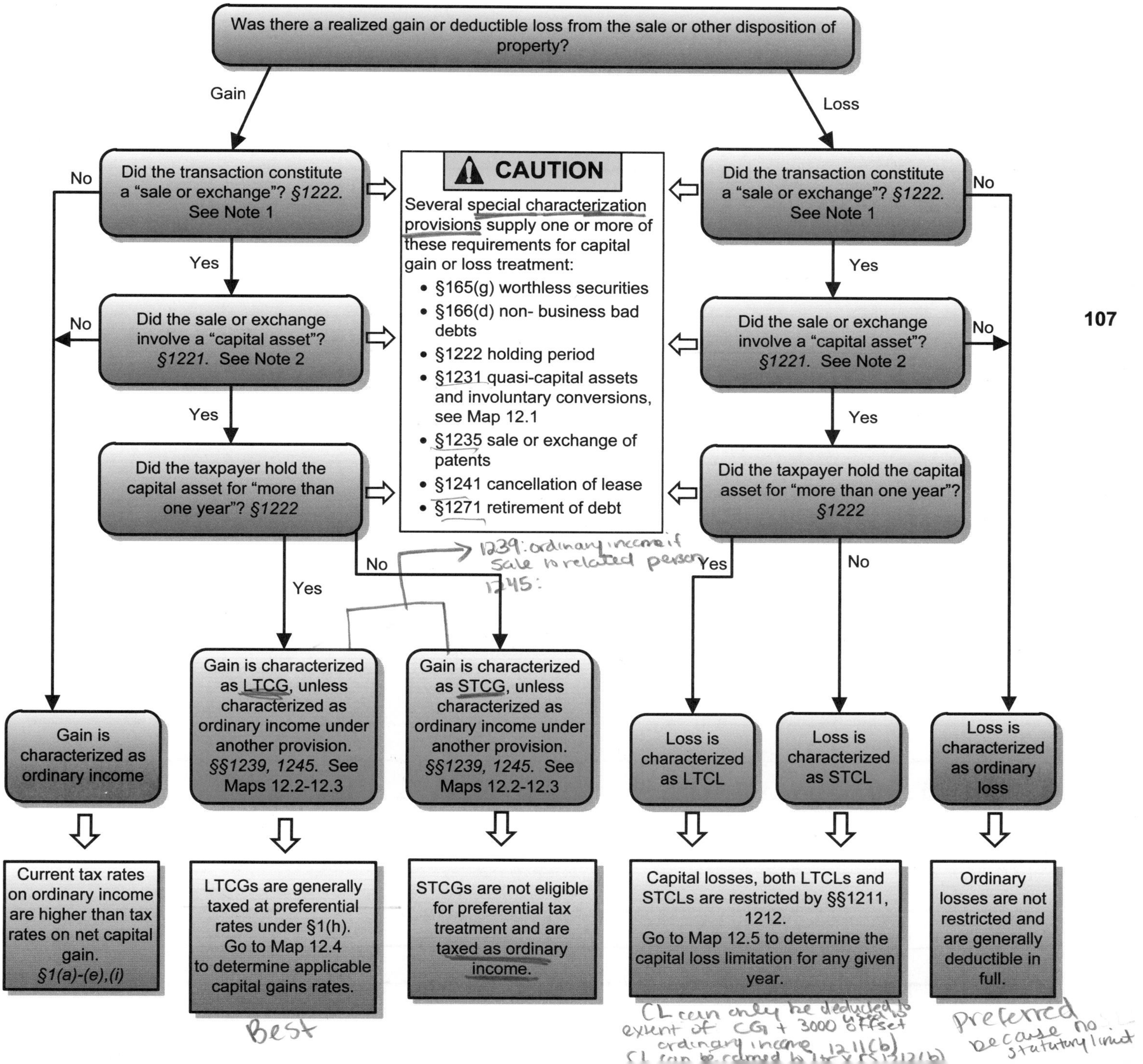

Was there a realized gain or deductible loss from the sale or other disposition of property?

Gain → / Loss →

Gain side:

Did the transaction constitute a "sale or exchange"? §1222. See Note 1 — No →

Yes ↓

Did the sale or exchange involve a "capital asset"? §1221. See Note 2 — No →

Yes ↓

Did the taxpayer hold the capital asset for "more than one year"? §1222

Yes ↓ / No →

⚠ **CAUTION**

Several special characterization provisions supply one or more of these requirements for capital gain or loss treatment:

- §165(g) worthless securities
- §166(d) non- business bad debts
- §1222 holding period
- §1231 quasi-capital assets and involuntary conversions, see Map 12.1
- §1235 sale or exchange of patents
- §1241 cancellation of lease
- §1271 retirement of debt

107

Loss side:

Did the transaction constitute a "sale or exchange"? §1222. See Note 1 — No →

Yes ↓

Did the sale or exchange involve a "capital asset"? §1221. See Note 2 — No →

Yes ↓

Did the taxpayer hold the capital asset for "more than one year"? §1222

Yes ↓ / No ↓

Bottom boxes:

Gain is characterized as ordinary income

Gain is characterized as LTCG, unless characterized as ordinary income under another provision. §§1239, 1245. See Maps 12.2-12.3

Gain is characterized as STCG, unless characterized as ordinary income under another provision. §§1239, 1245. See Maps 12.2-12.3

Loss is characterized as LTCL

Loss is characterized as STCL

Loss is characterized as ordinary loss

Final row:

Current tax rates on ordinary income are higher than tax rates on net capital gain. §1(a)-(e),(i)

LTCGs are generally taxed at preferential rates under §1(h). Go to Map 12.4 to determine applicable capital gains rates.

STCGs are not eligible for preferential tax treatment and are taxed as ordinary income.

Capital losses, both LTCLs and STCLs are restricted by §§1211, 1212. Go to Map 12.5 to determine the capital loss limitation for any given year.

Ordinary losses are not restricted and are generally deductible in full.

(handwritten annotations:)

1239: ordinary income if sale to related person
1245:

CL can only be deducted to extent of CG + 3000 offset ordinary income 1211(b)
CL can be carried b 1 + r 1212(b)

Preferred because no statutory limit

Best

Notes

Capital Gains and Losses
Overview
12.0 Notes

Note 1

The "Sale or Exchange" Requirement

A taxpayer's interest in property must be terminated in a special way—a sale or exchange—in order to qualify for capital gain or loss treatment. The words "sale or exchange" have broad meaning, and are not limited to the standard transfer of property by taxpayer to another for consideration in money or money's worth. Examples include:

- Transfer of appreciated property in satisfaction of a bequest. *Kenan v. Comm'r*

- Involuntary foreclosure sale of property. *Helvering v. Hammel*

- Conveyance of property to a mortgagee by a quitclaim deed in lieu of foreclosure. *Freeland v. Comm'r*

- Abandonment of property subject to nonrecourse mortgage. *Yarbro v. Comm'r*

Note 2

Definition of "Capital Asset"

A transaction must involve a "capital asset" in order to qualify for capital gain or loss treatment. §1221(a) defines the term capital asset as all property held by the taxpayer (whether or not connected with a trade or business), subject to several important exceptions:

- Inventory and inventory-like property. *§1221(a)(1)*

- Depreciable or real property used in taxpayer's trade or business. *§1221(a)(2)*

    - Includes land, buildings, and equipment used in business.

    - Also includes many forms of intangible property, including §197 intangibles. *§197(f)(7)*

    - Although not capital assets under §1221(a)(2), such property may qualify for capital treatment under §1231. See Map 12.1

- Self-created copyrights and similar property. *§1221(a)(3); §1.1221-1(c); but see §1221(b)(3) (special rule for musical copyrights)*

- Accounts receivable for service or inventory. *§1221(a)(4)*

- Federal publications. *§1221(a)(5)*

- Supplies used in a trade or business. *§1221(a)(8)*

Notes

Quasi-Capital Assets and Involuntary Conversions
12.1

Premise
§1231 is a special characterization provision that accords quasi-capital asset status to property excluded from the definition of capital asset (i.e., trade or business property). Likewise, §1231 also accords sale or exchange treatment to transactions that are not considered sales or exchanges (i.e., involuntary conversions). As this Map shows, the operation of §1231 requires a taxpayer to net all §1231 gains and losses that occur during the year to determine their character.

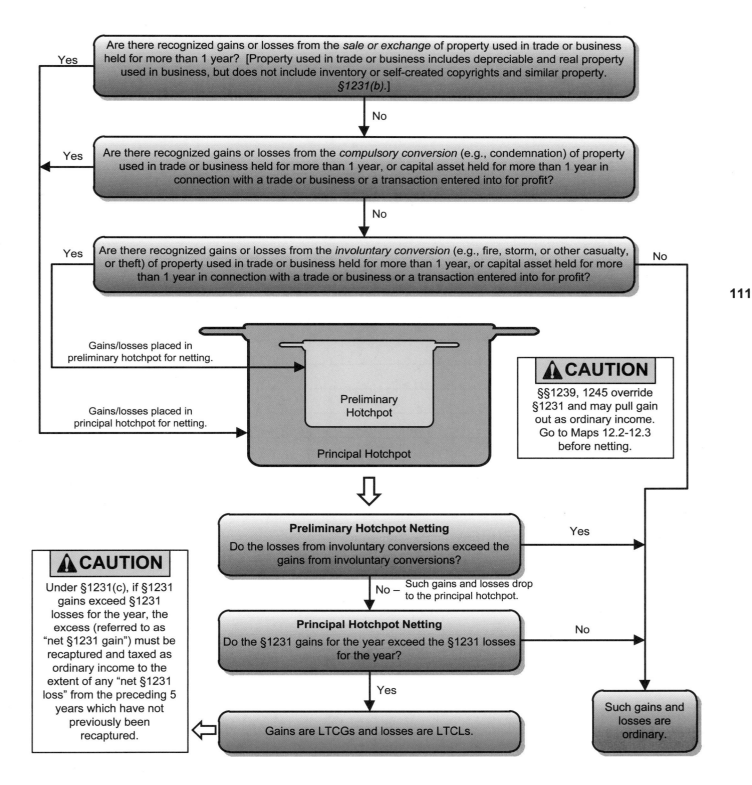

Yes — Are there recognized gains or losses from the *sale or exchange* of property used in trade or business held for more than 1 year? [Property used in trade or business includes depreciable and real property used in business, but does not include inventory or self-created copyrights and similar property. *§1231(b)*.]

No

Yes — Are there recognized gains or losses from the *compulsory conversion* (e.g., condemnation) of property used in trade or business held for more than 1 year, or capital asset held for more than 1 year in connection with a trade or business or a transaction entered into for profit?

No

Yes — Are there recognized gains or losses from the *involuntary conversion* (e.g., fire, storm, or other casualty, or theft) of property used in trade or business held for more than 1 year, or capital asset held for more than 1 year in connection with a trade or business or a transaction entered into for profit? — **No**

111

Gains/losses placed in preliminary hotchpot for netting.

Gains/losses placed in principal hotchpot for netting.

Preliminary Hotchpot

Principal Hotchpot

⚠ **CAUTION**
§§1239, 1245 override §1231 and may pull gain out as ordinary income. Go to Maps 12.2-12.3 before netting.

Preliminary Hotchpot Netting
Do the losses from involuntary conversions exceed the gains from involuntary conversions? — **Yes**

No – Such gains and losses drop to the principal hotchpot.

Principal Hotchpot Netting
Do the §1231 gains for the year exceed the §1231 losses for the year? — **No**

Yes

⚠ **CAUTION**
Under §1231(c), if §1231 gains exceed §1231 losses for the year, the excess (referred to as "net §1231 gain") must be recaptured and taxed as ordinary income to the extent of any "net §1231 loss" from the preceding 5 years which have not previously been recaptured.

Gains are LTCGs and losses are LTCLs.

Such gains and losses are ordinary.

112

Characterization Under §1239
12.2

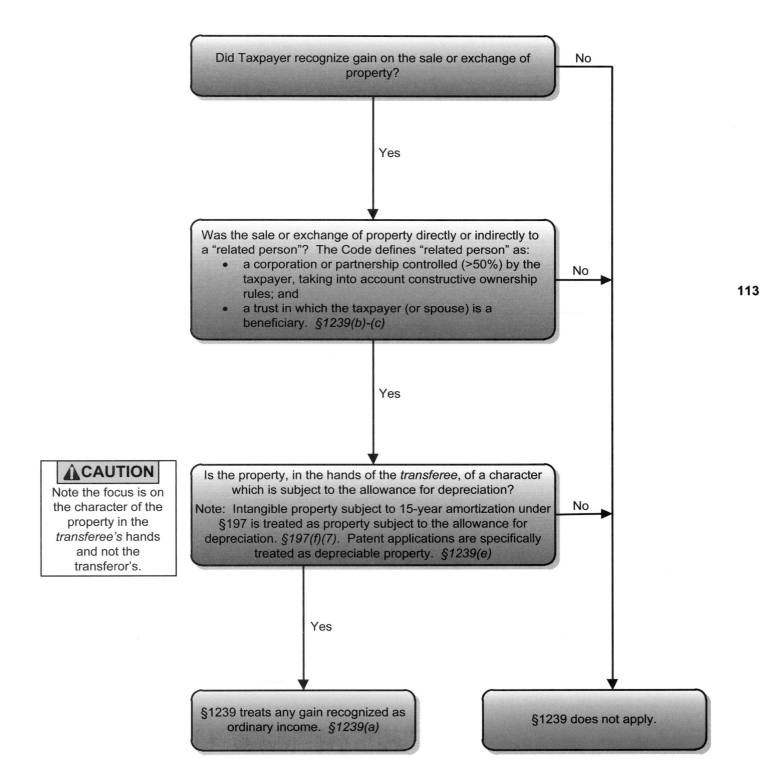

Premise

This Map addresses §1239, an overriding characterization rule requiring any gain recognized in certain transactions between related parties be treated as ordinary income. The purpose behind §1239 is to prevent taxpayers from selling low-basis, high-value depreciable property to a related party in order to step up the property's basis in the hands of the related transferee at the low cost of capital gains tax to the transferor.

Did Taxpayer recognize gain on the sale or exchange of property? — **No**

Yes

Was the sale or exchange of property directly or indirectly to a "related person"? The Code defines "related person" as:
- a corporation or partnership controlled (>50%) by the taxpayer, taking into account constructive ownership rules; and
- a trust in which the taxpayer (or spouse) is a beneficiary. *§1239(b)-(c)* — **No**

Yes

⚠ CAUTION

Note the focus is on the character of the property in the *transferee's* hands and not the transferor's.

Is the property, in the hands of the *transferee*, of a character which is subject to the allowance for depreciation?

Note: Intangible property subject to 15-year amortization under §197 is treated as property subject to the allowance for depreciation. *§197(f)(7)*. Patent applications are specifically treated as depreciable property. *§1239(e)* — **No**

Yes

§1239 treats any gain recognized as ordinary income. *§1239(a)*

§1239 does not apply.

Notes

Recapture of Depreciation Under §1245
12.3

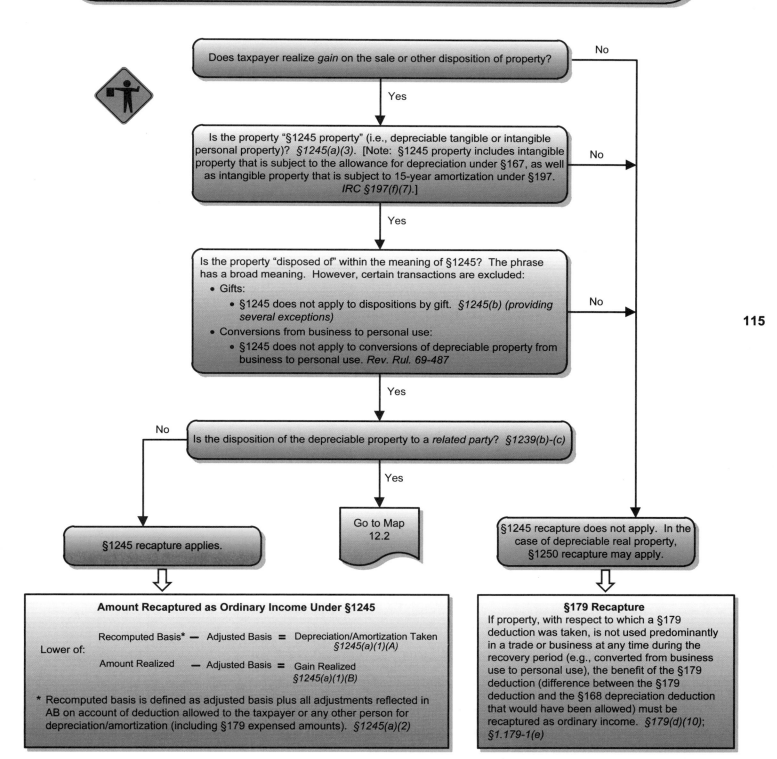

Premise
This Map considers §1245, an overriding provision that treats gain attributable to depreciation deductions as ordinary income whenever "§1245 property" is "disposed of."

Does taxpayer realize *gain* on the sale or other disposition of property? — **No**

Yes

Is the property "§1245 property" (i.e., depreciable tangible or intangible personal property)? *§1245(a)(3)*. [Note: §1245 property includes intangible property that is subject to the allowance for depreciation under §167, as well as intangible property that is subject to 15-year amortization under §197. *IRC §197(f)(7)*.] — **No**

Yes

Is the property "disposed of" within the meaning of §1245? The phrase has a broad meaning. However, certain transactions are excluded:
- Gifts:
  - §1245 does not apply to dispositions by gift. *§1245(b) (providing several exceptions)*
- Conversions from business to personal use:
  - §1245 does not apply to conversions of depreciable property from business to personal use. *Rev. Rul. 69-487* — **No**

Yes

No — Is the disposition of the depreciable property to a *related party*? *§1239(b)-(c)*

Yes

§1245 recapture applies.

Go to Map 12.2

§1245 recapture does not apply. In the case of depreciable real property, §1250 recapture may apply.

Amount Recaptured as Ordinary Income Under §1245

Lower of:

Recomputed Basis* — Adjusted Basis = Depreciation/Amortization Taken
§1245(a)(1)(A)

Amount Realized — Adjusted Basis = Gain Realized
§1245(a)(1)(B)

* Recomputed basis is defined as adjusted basis plus all adjustments reflected in AB on account of deduction allowed to the taxpayer or any other person for depreciation/amortization (including §179 expensed amounts). *§1245(a)(2)*

§179 Recapture
If property, with respect to which a §179 deduction was taken, is not used predominantly in a trade or business at any time during the recovery period (e.g., converted from business use to personal use), the benefit of the §179 deduction (difference between the §179 deduction and the §168 depreciation deduction that would have been allowed) must be recaptured as ordinary income. *§179(d)(10); §1.179-1(e)*

Notes

116

Tax Rates on Net Capital Gains
12.4

Premise

Tax rate preference comes into play only if a taxpayer has a "net capital gain" (NCG) for the year, which is possible only if taxpayer has some "long-term capital gain" (LTCG) for the year. *§1(h)*. This Map determines the applicable tax rate on NCG, which depends on several factors, including the nature of the asset producing long-term capital gain and the taxpayer's ordinary tax bracket.

⚠ **CAUTION**

This Map provides the capital gains rates in existence at the time of publication of this book.

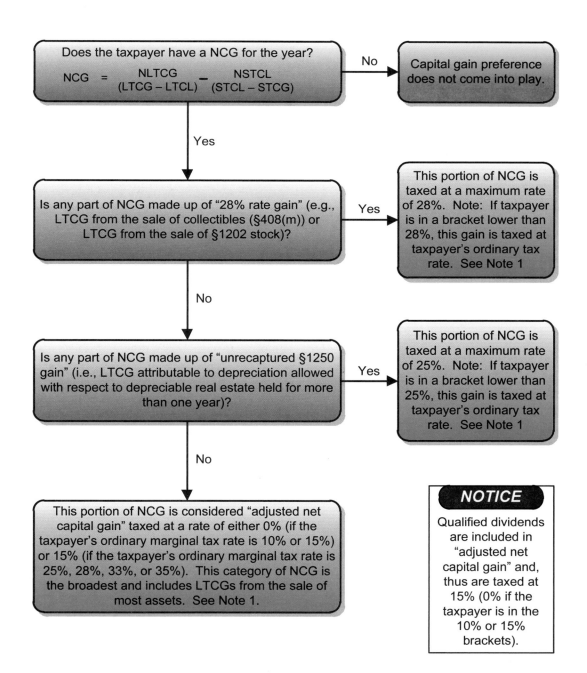

Does the taxpayer have a NCG for the year?

$$NCG = \underset{(LTCG - LTCL)}{NLTCG} - \underset{(STCL - STCG)}{NSTCL}$$

No → Capital gain preference does not come into play.

Yes ↓

Is any part of NCG made up of "28% rate gain" (e.g., LTCG from the sale of collectibles (§408(m)) or LTCG from the sale of §1202 stock)?

Yes → This portion of NCG is taxed at a maximum rate of 28%. Note: If taxpayer is in a bracket lower than 28%, this gain is taxed at taxpayer's ordinary tax rate. See Note 1

No ↓

Is any part of NCG made up of "unrecaptured §1250 gain" (i.e., LTCG attributable to depreciation allowed with respect to depreciable real estate held for more than one year)?

Yes → This portion of NCG is taxed at a maximum rate of 25%. Note: If taxpayer is in a bracket lower than 25%, this gain is taxed at taxpayer's ordinary tax rate. See Note 1

No ↓

This portion of NCG is considered "adjusted net capital gain" taxed at a rate of either 0% (if the taxpayer's ordinary marginal tax rate is 10% or 15%) or 15% (if the taxpayer's ordinary marginal tax rate is 25%, 28%, 33%, or 35%). This category of NCG is the broadest and includes LTCGs from the sale of most assets. See Note 1.

NOTICE

Qualified dividends are included in "adjusted net capital gain" and, thus are taxed at 15% (0% if the taxpayer is in the 10% or 15% brackets).

117

Notes

Tax Rates on Net Capital Gains
12.4 Notes

Note 1

As Map 12.4 illustrates, to determine the proper rate applicable to NCG, a taxpayer must first determine her marginal rate on ordinary income. The taxpayer must then layer her net capital gain.

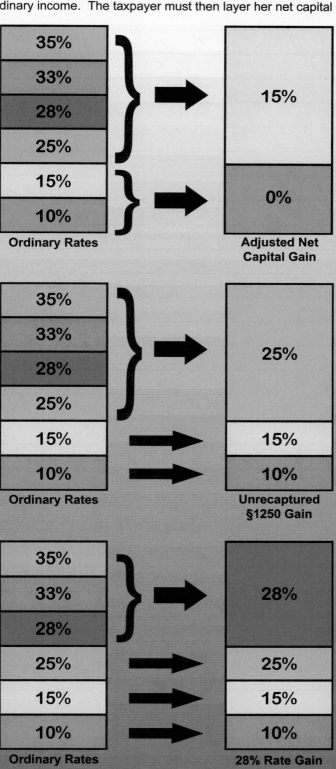

Notes

Capital Loss Limitation Rules
12.5

Premise

This Map addresses the statutory limitation on capital loss deductions by individuals (§1211(b)) and the character of carryover losses into subsequent years (§1212(b)).

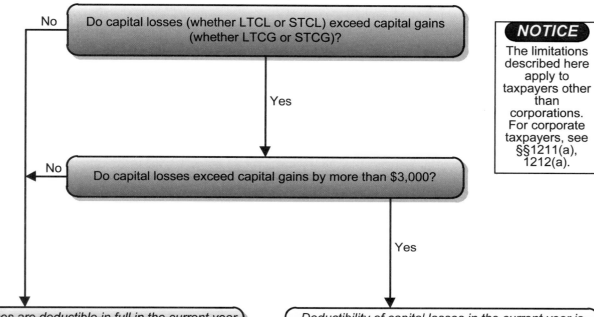

No — Do capital losses (whether LTCL or STCL) exceed capital gains (whether LTCG or STCG)?

Yes

No — Do capital losses exceed capital gains by more than $3,000?

Yes

NOTICE

The limitations described here apply to taxpayers other than corporations. For corporate taxpayers, see §§1211(a), 1212(a).

121

Capital losses are deductible in full in the current year. Here capital losses will offset capital gains in the current year; if capital losses exceed capital gains the excess (up to $3,000) will offset ordinary income in the current year.

Deductibility of capital losses in the current year is limited: Capital losses will offset capital gains plus $3,000 of ordinary income. Unused capital losses are carried forward and can be deducted in future years subject to the same limitations described in this Map.

Capital Loss Allocation Rules

If capital gains exceed capital losses, taxpayer may be entitled to preferential rate treatment on the excess. Because LTCGs are taxed at varying rates depending on the nature of the asset sold, it may be necessary to determine which capital losses offset which capital gains. The loss allocation rules are as follows:

- STCLs are applied to reduce STCGs. Any excess (NSTCL) is first applied to reduce LTCG taxed at 28%, then LTCG taxed at 25%, then LTCG taxed at 15%.

- LTCLs are allocated to their related category of LTCGs.

Character of Capital Loss Carryovers

$$\underset{\text{(STCL - STCG*)}}{\text{NSTCL}} \quad - \quad \underset{\text{(LTCG - LTCL)}}{\text{NLTCG}} \quad = \quad \text{STCL c/o}$$

$$\underset{\text{(LTCL - LTCG)}}{\text{NLTCL}} \quad - \quad \underset{\text{(STCG* - STCL)}}{\text{NSTCG}} \quad = \quad \text{LTCL c/o}$$

* The Code creates a $3,000 constructive STCG for purposes of these formulas. *§1212(b)(2)*. The effect of this provision is to cause STCLs to be used first to offset the $3,000 of ordinary income permitted by §1211.

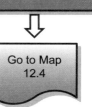

Go to Map 12.4

Notes

122

Like Kind Exchanges
13.0

Y

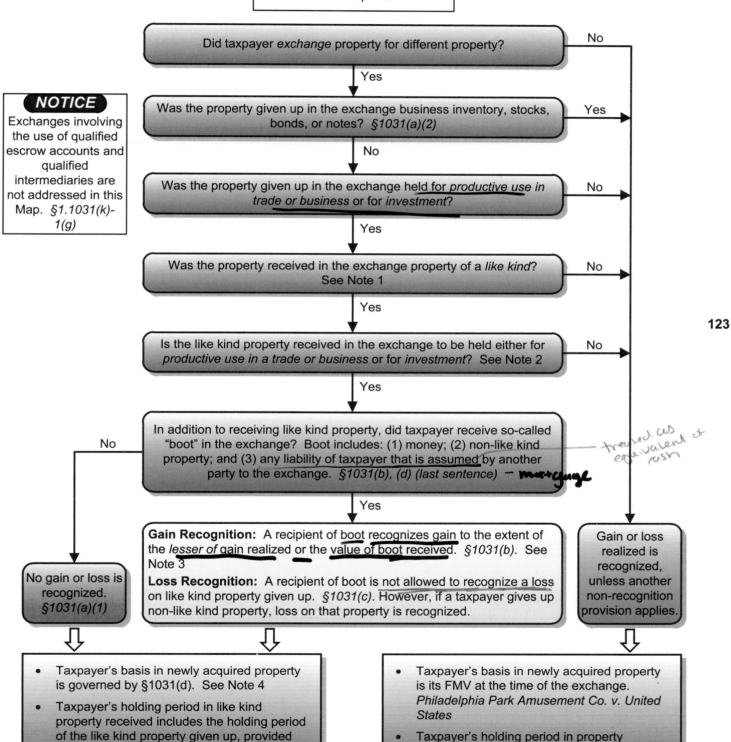

⚠ WARNING

You should not begin with this Map. You should be directed here from Map 3.0.

Did taxpayer *exchange* property for different property? — **No**

↓ **Yes**

NOTICE

Exchanges involving the use of qualified escrow accounts and qualified intermediaries are not addressed in this Map. *§1.1031(k)-1(g)*

Was the property given up in the exchange business inventory, stocks, bonds, or notes? *§1031(a)(2)* — **Yes**

↓ **No**

Was the property given up in the exchange held for *productive use in trade or business* or for *investment*? — **No**

↓ **Yes**

Was the property received in the exchange property of a *like kind*? See Note 1 — **No**

↓ **Yes**

123

Is the like kind property received in the exchange to be held either for *productive use in a trade or business* or for *investment*? See Note 2 — **No**

↓ **Yes**

No — In addition to receiving like kind property, did taxpayer receive so-called "boot" in the exchange? Boot includes: (1) money; (2) non-like kind property; and (3) any liability of taxpayer that is assumed by another party to the exchange. *§1031(b), (d) (last sentence)* — *mortgage*

treated as equivalent of cash

↓ **Yes**

No gain or loss is recognized. *§1031(a)(1)*

Gain Recognition: A recipient of boot recognizes gain to the extent of the *lesser of* gain realized or the value of boot received. *§1031(b)*. See Note 3

Loss Recognition: A recipient of boot is not allowed to recognize a loss on like kind property given up. *§1031(c)*. However, if a taxpayer gives up non-like kind property, loss on that property is recognized.

Gain or loss realized is recognized, unless another non-recognition provision applies.

⇩

- Taxpayer's basis in newly acquired property is governed by §1031(d). See Note 4
- Taxpayer's holding period in like kind property received includes the holding period of the like kind property given up, provided the latter is either a capital asset or §1231 property. *§1223(1)*

⇩

- Taxpayer's basis in newly acquired property is its FMV at the time of the exchange. *Philadelphia Park Amusement Co. v. United States*
- Taxpayer's holding period in property received starts right away (tacking does not apply).

Notes

Like Kind Exchanges
13.0 Notes

Y

Note 1

- The words "like kind" have reference to the nature or character of the property and not to its grade or quality. *§1.1031(a)-1(b)*
  - *Real estate* for real estate, however improved, is considered like kind. *§1.1031(a)-1(b)*
  - *Depreciable tangible personal property* meets the like kind requirement if exchanged for property that is either like kind or of a "like class" (i.e., within the same General Asset Class of Rev. Proc. 87-56). *§1.1031(a)-2(b)*
  - Whether *intangible personal property* is of a like kind to other intangible personal property generally depends on the nature or character of the rights involved (e.g., patent or a copyright) and also on the nature or character of the underlying property to which the intangible personal property relates. *§1.1031(a)-2(c)*
- Property received will not be treated as like kind property if certain timing rules are not met. Those rules require that the taxpayer must *identify* the replacement property within 45 days after the transfer of the property given up, and the replacement property must be received within 180 days after taxpayer transfers the property given up. *§1031(a)(3)*
- Recall from Map 12.3 that §1245 (the depreciation recapture rule) overrides all other Code sections. §1245(b)(4), however, provides that §1245 will not override §1031 as long as the property received in the exchange is also §1245 property. Thus, if taxpayer exchanges a truck used in her business for another truck to be used in her business, no §1245 recapture will occur.

Note 2

A taxpayer is within §1031 if she exchanges *investment* property for *business* property or vice versa. *§1.1031(a)-1(a)*

Note 3

In most regards, assumption of liability is treated as the equivalent of cash for purposes of determining boot under §1031. *§1031(d) last sentence.* When assumptions of liability pass in both directions, they are netted, so only the transferor with the greater liability has boot. *§1.1031(d)-2 (providing net liability relief is treated as boot).* An assumption of liability cannot offset cash received for boot purposes, but cash paid can offset an assumption of liability for boot purposes. *Id.*

Note 4

Basis in Property Given Up (cost)

- Money Received*

+ Gain Recognized

- Loss Recognized

_____

Basis in Property Received
§1031(d)

*(net liability relief treated as money received. *§1031(d) (last sentence); §1.1031(d)-2)*

see like-kind
for examples w/
boot, cash +
mortgages

Notes

Involuntary Conversions
13.1

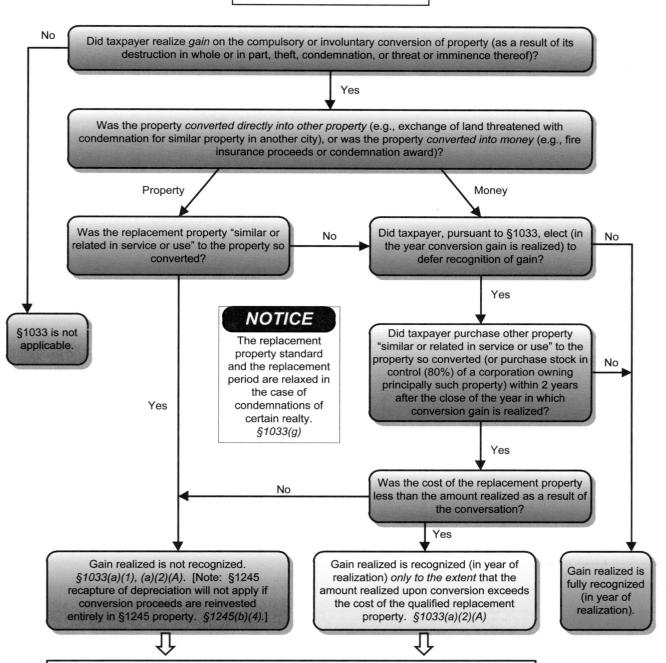

⚠ WARNING

You should not begin with this Map. You should be directed here from Map 3.0.

Did taxpayer realize *gain* on the compulsory or involuntary conversion of property (as a result of its destruction in whole or in part, theft, condemnation, or threat or imminence thereof)?

No → §1033 is not applicable.

Yes ↓

Was the property *converted directly into other property* (e.g., exchange of land threatened with condemnation for similar property in another city), or was the property *converted into money* (e.g., fire insurance proceeds or condemnation award)?

Property → Was the replacement property "similar or related in service or use" to the property so converted?

Money → Did taxpayer, pursuant to §1033, elect (in the year conversion gain is realized) to defer recognition of gain?

No → (from replacement property question)

No → Gain realized is fully recognized (in year of realization).

Yes → Did taxpayer purchase other property "similar or related in service or use" to the property so converted (or purchase stock in control (80%) of a corporation owning principally such property) within 2 years after the close of the year in which conversion gain is realized?

No → Gain realized is fully recognized (in year of realization).

NOTICE

The replacement property standard and the replacement period are relaxed in the case of condemnations of certain realty. *§1033(g)*

Yes ↓

Was the cost of the replacement property less than the amount realized as a result of the conversation?

No → Gain realized is not recognized.

Yes → Gain realized is recognized (in year of realization) *only to the extent* that the amount realized upon conversion exceeds the cost of the qualified replacement property. *§1033(a)(2)(A)*

Gain realized is not recognized. *§1033(a)(1), (a)(2)(A).* [Note: §1245 recapture of depreciation will not apply if conversion proceeds are reinvested entirely in §1245 property. *§1245(b)(4)*.]

Basis: If property is converted into similar-use property and gain is not recognized , then basis of the replacement property is the same as taxpayer's basis in the converted property. *§1033(b)(1)*. If property is converted into money and taxpayer elects not to recognize gain, then the basis of the replacement property is its cost less any unrecognized gain. *§1033(b)(2)*

Holding Period: The holding period of the replacement property includes the holding period of the property converted if the latter was a capital asset at the time of conversion. *Rev. Rul. 72-451*

Notes

Transfers of Property Between Spouses or Incident to Divorce
13.2

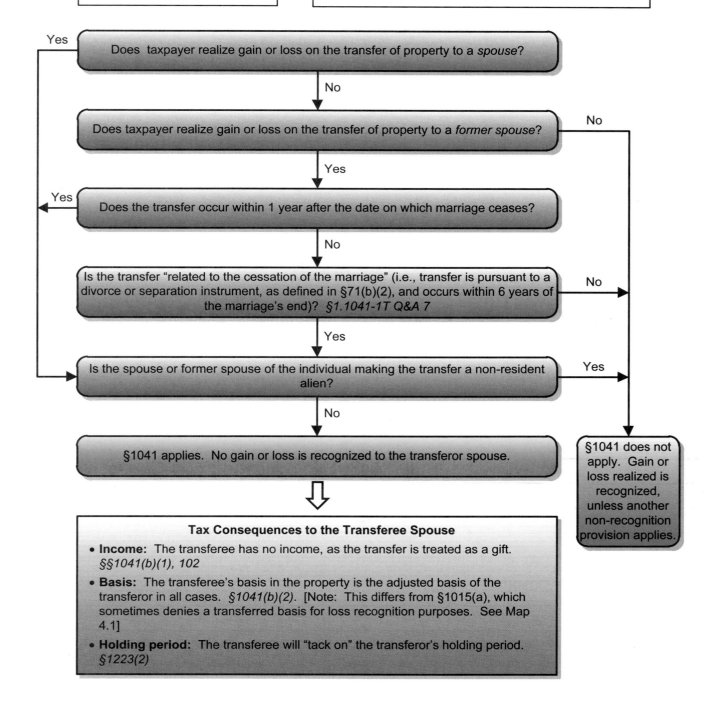

Premise

This Map addresses §1041, which governs transfers of property between spouses or former spouses incident to divorce. It impacts *transferors* (no gain or loss recognition) as well as *transferees* (no income and a transferred basis).

⚠ WARNING

You should not begin with this Map. You should be directed here from Map 3.0 or 3.1.

NOTICE

Under limited circumstances, a transfer of property to a third party can qualify for §1041 treatment. *§1.1041-1T(c) Q&A 9*. For divorce-related redemptions of stock, see Note 1.

Does taxpayer realize gain or loss on the transfer of property to a *spouse*? — Yes

No

Does taxpayer realize gain or loss on the transfer of property to a *former spouse*? — No

Yes

Does the transfer occur within 1 year after the date on which marriage ceases? — Yes

No

Is the transfer "related to the cessation of the marriage" (i.e., transfer is pursuant to a divorce or separation instrument, as defined in §71(b)(2), and occurs within 6 years of the marriage's end)? *§1.1041-1T Q&A 7* — No

Yes

Is the spouse or former spouse of the individual making the transfer a non-resident alien? — Yes

No

§1041 applies. No gain or loss is recognized to the transferor spouse.

§1041 does not apply. Gain or loss realized is recognized, unless another non-recognition provision applies.

Tax Consequences to the Transferee Spouse

- **Income:** The transferee has no income, as the transfer is treated as a gift. *§§1041(b)(1), 102*
- **Basis:** The transferee's basis in the property is the adjusted basis of the transferor in all cases. *§1041(b)(2)*. [Note: This differs from §1015(a), which sometimes denies a transferred basis for loss recognition purposes. See Map 4.1]
- **Holding period:** The transferee will "tack on" the transferor's holding period. *§1223(2)*

Notes

Transfers of Property Between Spouses or Incident to Divorce
13.2 Notes

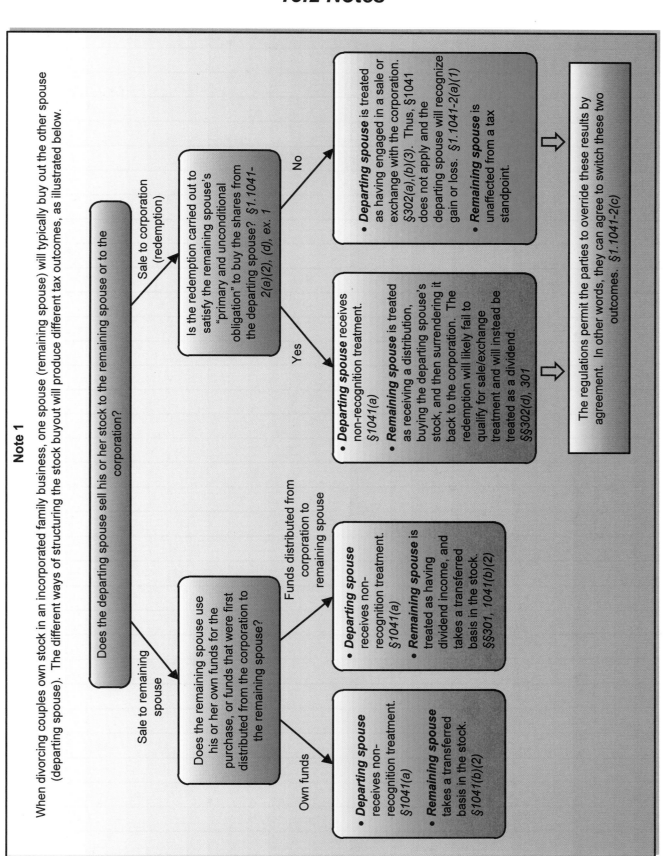

Note 1

When divorcing couples own stock in an incorporated family business, one spouse (remaining spouse) will typically buy out the other spouse (departing spouse). The different ways of structuring the stock buyout will produce different tax outcomes, as illustrated below.

Does the departing spouse sell his or her stock to the remaining spouse or to the corporation?

Sale to remaining spouse

Does the remaining spouse use his or her own funds for the purchase, or funds that were first distributed from the corporation to the remaining spouse?

Own funds

- *Departing spouse* receives non-recognition treatment. §1041(a)
- *Remaining spouse* takes a transferred basis in the stock. §1041(b)(2)

Funds distributed from corporation to remaining spouse

- *Departing spouse* receives non-recognition treatment. §1041(a)
- *Remaining spouse* is treated as having dividend income, and takes a transferred basis in the stock. §§301, 1041(b)(2)

Sale to corporation (redemption)

Is the redemption carried out to satisfy the remaining spouse's "primary and unconditional obligation" to buy the shares from the departing spouse? §1.1041-2(a)(2), (d), ex. 1

Yes

- *Departing spouse* receives non-recognition treatment. §1041(a)
- *Remaining spouse* is treated as receiving a distribution, buying the departing spouse's stock, and then surrendering it back to the corporation. The redemption will likely fail to qualify for sale/exchange treatment and will instead be treated as a dividend. §§302(d), 301

No

- *Departing spouse* is treated as having engaged in a sale or exchange with the corporation. §302(a), (b)(3). Thus, §1041 does not apply and the departing spouse will recognize gain or loss. §1.1041-2(a)(1)
- *Remaining spouse* is unaffected from a tax standpoint.

The regulations permit the parties to override these results by agreement. In other words, they can agree to switch these two outcomes. §1.1041-2(c)

131

Notes

132

Corporate Formations
13.3

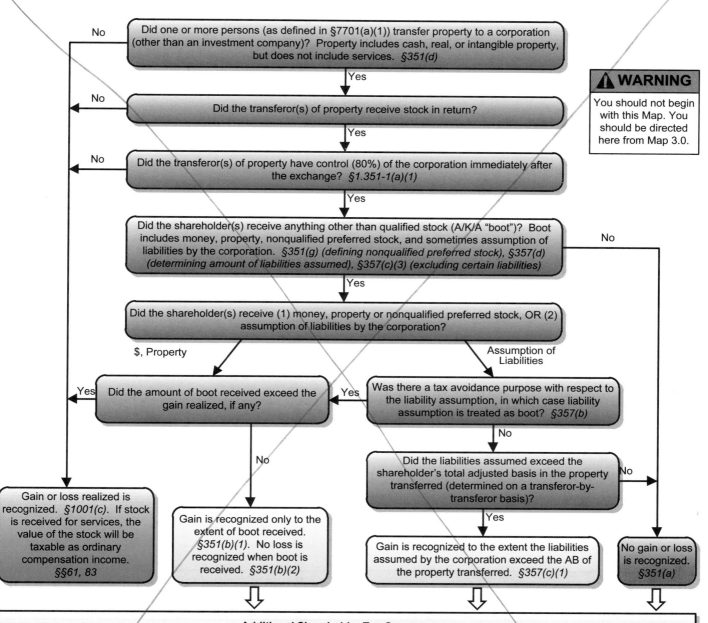

Did one or more persons (as defined in §7701(a)(1)) transfer property to a corporation (other than an investment company)? Property includes cash, real, or intangible property, but does not include services. §351(d)

— No →

↓ Yes

Did the transferor(s) of property receive stock in return?

— No →

↓ Yes

Did the transferor(s) of property have control (80%) of the corporation immediately after the exchange? §1.351-1(a)(1)

— No →

↓ Yes

Did the shareholder(s) receive anything other than qualified stock (A/K/A "boot")? Boot includes money, property, nonqualified preferred stock, and sometimes assumption of liabilities by the corporation. §351(g) (defining nonqualified preferred stock), §357(d) (determining amount of liabilities assumed), §357(c)(3) (excluding certain liabilities)

— No →

↓ Yes

Did the shareholder(s) receive (1) money, property or nonqualified preferred stock, OR (2) assumption of liabilities by the corporation?

→ $, Property

→ Assumption of Liabilities

Did the amount of boot received exceed the gain realized, if any? — Yes →

↓ No

Was there a tax avoidance purpose with respect to the liability assumption, in which case liability assumption is treated as boot? §357(b) — Yes →

↓ No

Did the liabilities assumed exceed the shareholder's total adjusted basis in the property transferred (determined on a transferor-by-transferor basis)? — No →

↓ Yes

Gain or loss realized is recognized. §1001(c). If stock is received for services, the value of the stock will be taxable as ordinary compensation income. §§61, 83

Gain is recognized only to the extent of boot received. §351(b)(1). No loss is recognized when boot is received. §351(b)(2)

Gain is recognized to the extent the liabilities assumed by the corporation exceed the AB of the property transferred. §357(c)(1)

No gain or loss is recognized. §351(a)

> ⚠ **WARNING**
>
> You should not begin with this Map. You should be directed here from Map 3.0.

133

Additional Shareholder Tax Consequences

- Character of gain recognized, if any, is usually capital gain as stock is held as a capital asset. See Map 12.0

- Basis of the qualified stock received equals the basis in the property given minus boot received (money, other property, debt relief) plus gain recognized. §358(a)(1), (d)(1)

- Holding period of the qualified stock received includes the holding period of the property given provided it was a capital asset or §1231 property. §1223(1)

- Basis of boot property received equals its fair market value. §358(a)(2). Tacking does not apply.

Corporate Level Tax Consequences

- No gain or loss is recognized. §1032

- Basis of the property acquired equals the transferor's basis plus gain recognized to the transferor. §362(a). However, the corporation's aggregate bases in the assets cannot exceed the FMV of such property. §362(e)

Notes

Partnership Formations
13.4

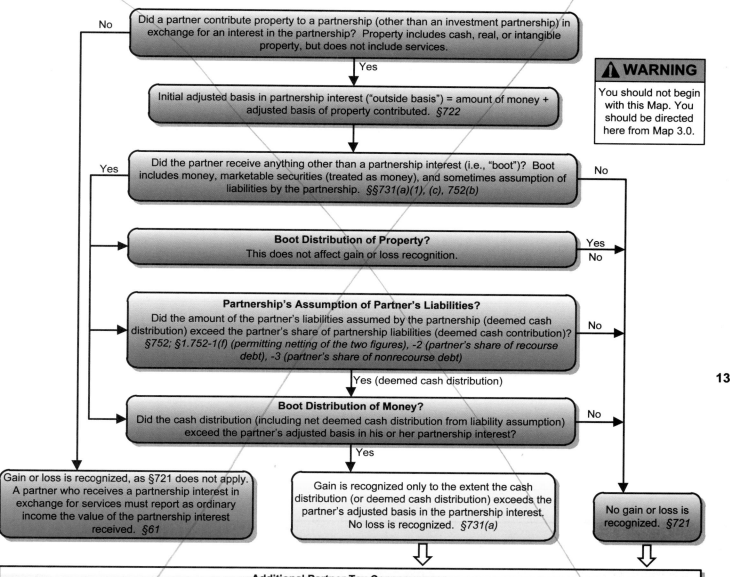

Did a partner contribute property to a partnership (other than an investment partnership) in exchange for an interest in the partnership? Property includes cash, real, or intangible property, but does not include services.

No →

Yes ↓

Initial adjusted basis in partnership interest ("outside basis") = amount of money + adjusted basis of property contributed. §722

⚠ **WARNING**

You should not begin with this Map. You should be directed here from Map 3.0.

Did the partner receive anything other than a partnership interest (i.e., "boot")? Boot includes money, marketable securities (treated as money), and sometimes assumption of liabilities by the partnership. §§731(a)(1), (c), 752(b)

Yes ← / **No** →

Boot Distribution of Property?
This does not affect gain or loss recognition.

Yes / **No**

Partnership's Assumption of Partner's Liabilities?
Did the amount of the partner's liabilities assumed by the partnership (deemed cash distribution) exceed the partner's share of partnership liabilities (deemed cash contribution)? §752; §1.752-1(f) (permitting netting of the two figures), -2 (partner's share of recourse debt), -3 (partner's share of nonrecourse debt)

No →

Yes (deemed cash distribution) ↓

135

Boot Distribution of Money?
Did the cash distribution (including net deemed cash distribution from liability assumption) exceed the partner's adjusted basis in his or her partnership interest?

No →

Yes ↓

Gain or loss is recognized, as §721 does not apply. A partner who receives a partnership interest in exchange for services must report as ordinary income the value of the partnership interest received. §61

Gain is recognized only to the extent the cash distribution (or deemed cash distribution) exceeds the partner's adjusted basis in the partnership interest. No loss is recognized. §731(a)

No gain or loss is recognized. §721

Additional Partner Tax Consequences

- Gain recognized as a result of a boot distribution is typically characterized as capital gain unless the partnership has a lot of inventory or accounts receivable. §§741, 751
- Partner's adjusted basis in boot property received is generally its adjusted basis to the partnership immediately before such distribution. §732
- Partner's adjusted basis in the partnership interest is the initial "outside basis" (determined by reference to basis of property contributed), reduced (but not below zero) by (1) the amount of any money distributed to such partner and (2) the adjusted basis to such partner of distributed property other than money. §733
- Partner's holding period in the partnership interest received generally includes the holding period of the property given up. §1223(1)

Partnership Level Tax Consequences

- No gain or loss is recognized to a partnership that receives property in exchange for its partnership interests. §721(a)
- Partnership's basis in any property received ("inside basis") is the same as the transferor partner's basis. §723
- Partnership's holding period in such property includes the holding period of the transferor partner. §1223(2)

Notes

Tax Computations
Overview
14.0

Premise
Once taxable income is determined, tax rates are applied to determine a tentative (pre-credits) tax liability. There are two rate structures: the ordinary income rate structure and the net capital gains rate structure. Then, pre-credits tax liability is reduced by various credits to determine a final tax liability. This Map references other Maps to consult when converting taxable income into a final tax liability.

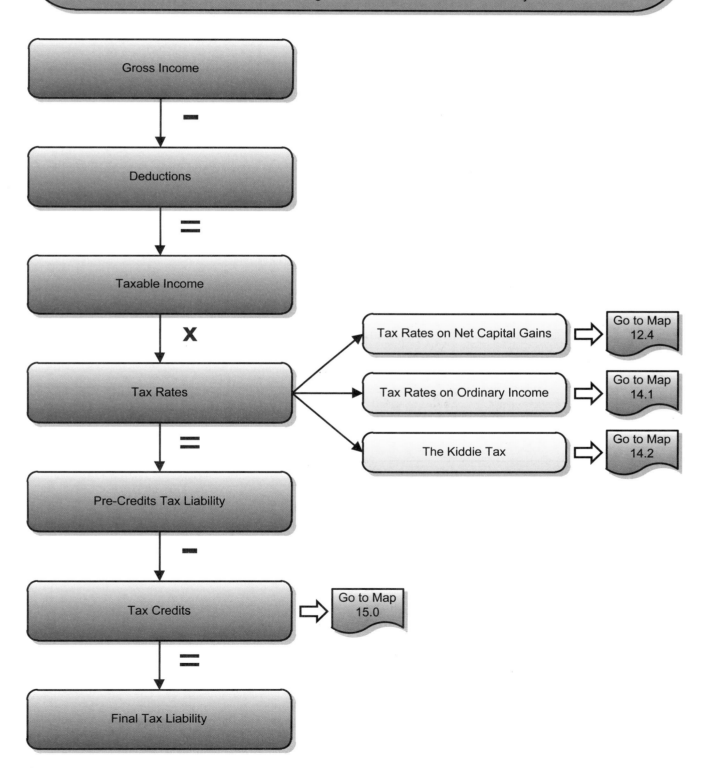

Gross Income

—

Deductions

=

Taxable Income

X

Tax Rates

Tax Rates on Net Capital Gains	Go to Map 12.4
Tax Rates on Ordinary Income	Go to Map 14.1
The Kiddie Tax	Go to Map 14.2

=

Pre-Credits Tax Liability

—

Tax Credits → Go to Map 15.0

=

Final Tax Liability

Notes

Ordinary Tax Rates and Taxpayer Classification
14.1

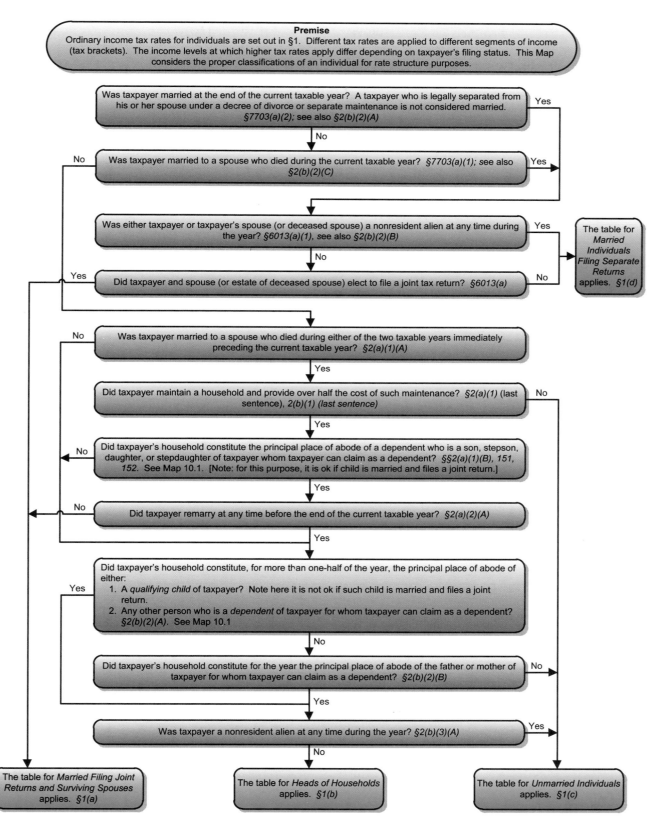

Premise
Ordinary income tax rates for individuals are set out in §1. Different tax rates are applied to different segments of income (tax brackets). The income levels at which higher tax rates apply differ depending on taxpayer's filing status. This Map considers the proper classifications of an individual for rate structure purposes.

Was taxpayer married at the end of the current taxable year? A taxpayer who is legally separated from his or her spouse under a decree of divorce or separate maintenance is not considered married. §7703(a)(2); see also §2(b)(2)(A) — Yes

No

Was taxpayer married to a spouse who died during the current taxable year? §7703(a)(1); see also §2(b)(2)(C) — Yes

No

Was either taxpayer or taxpayer's spouse (or deceased spouse) a nonresident alien at any time during the year? §6013(a)(1), see also §2(b)(2)(B) — Yes

No

Did taxpayer and spouse (or estate of deceased spouse) elect to file a joint tax return? §6013(a) — No

Yes

The table for *Married Individuals Filing Separate Returns* applies. §1(d)

Was taxpayer married to a spouse who died during either of the two taxable years immediately preceding the current taxable year? §2(a)(1)(A) — No

Yes

Did taxpayer maintain a household and provide over half the cost of such maintenance? §2(a)(1) (last sentence), 2(b)(1) (last sentence) — No

Yes

Did taxpayer's household constitute the principal place of abode of a dependent who is a son, stepson, daughter, or stepdaughter of taxpayer whom taxpayer can claim as a dependent? §§2(a)(1)(B), 151, 152. See Map 10.1. [Note: for this purpose, it is ok if child is married and files a joint return.] — No

Yes

Did taxpayer remarry at any time before the end of the current taxable year? §2(a)(2)(A) — No

Yes

Did taxpayer's household constitute, for more than one-half of the year, the principal place of abode of either:
1. A *qualifying child* of taxpayer? Note here it is not ok if such child is married and files a joint return.
2. Any other person who is a *dependent* of taxpayer for whom taxpayer can claim as a dependent? §2(b)(2)(A). See Map 10.1 — Yes

No

Did taxpayer's household constitute for the year the principal place of abode of the father or mother of taxpayer for whom taxpayer can claim as a dependent? §2(b)(2)(B) — No

Yes

Was taxpayer a nonresident alien at any time during the year? §2(b)(3)(A) — Yes

No

The table for *Married Filing Joint Returns and Surviving Spouses* applies. §1(a)

The table for *Heads of Households* applies. §1(b)

The table for *Unmarried Individuals* applies. §1(c)

139

Joint and Several Liability
When spouses file a joint return they are jointly and severally liable for the tax liability. §6013(d)(3). For spousal relief provisions, see §§66, 6015.

The Kiddie Tax
If taxpayer is under the age of 18, his or her unearned income may be subject to tax at his or her parent's top tax rate. See Map 14.2

Notes

The Kiddie Tax
14.2

Premise
This Map considers §1(g), which prevents income-shifting to a child by taxing the child's net unearned income at the parent's top tax rate.

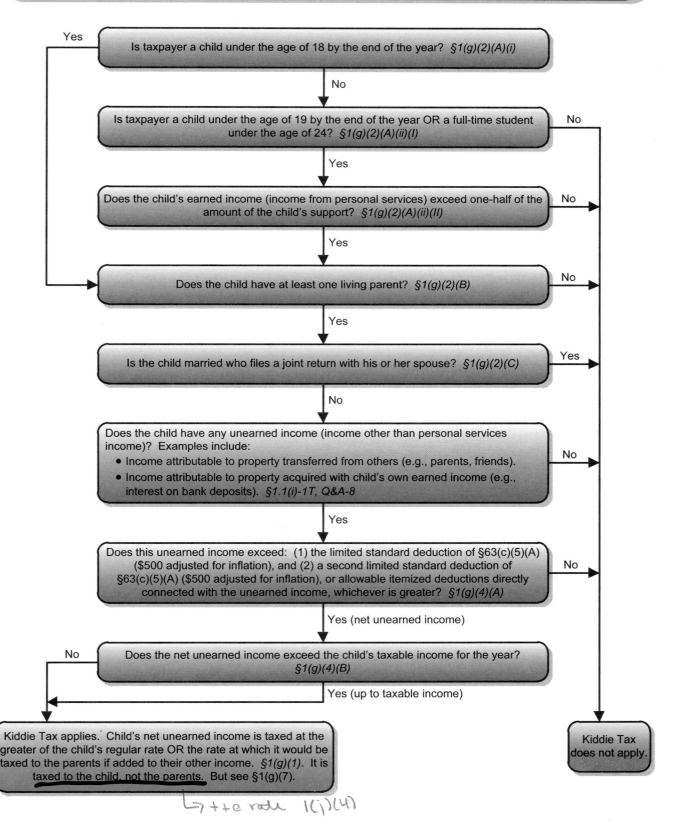

Is taxpayer a child under the age of 18 by the end of the year? *§1(g)(2)(A)(i)*
→ Yes

No ↓

Is taxpayer a child under the age of 19 by the end of the year OR a full-time student under the age of 24? *§1(g)(2)(A)(ii)(I)*
→ No

Yes ↓

Does the child's earned income (income from personal services) exceed one-half of the amount of the child's support? *§1(g)(2)(A)(ii)(II)*
→ No

Yes ↓

Does the child have at least one living parent? *§1(g)(2)(B)*
→ No

Yes ↓

Is the child married who files a joint return with his or her spouse? *§1(g)(2)(C)*
→ Yes

No ↓

Does the child have any unearned income (income other than personal services income)? Examples include:
- Income attributable to property transferred from others (e.g., parents, friends).
- Income attributable to property acquired with child's own earned income (e.g., interest on bank deposits). *§1.1(i)-1T, Q&A-8*
→ No

Yes ↓

Does this unearned income exceed: (1) the limited standard deduction of §63(c)(5)(A) ($500 adjusted for inflation), and (2) a second limited standard deduction of §63(c)(5)(A) ($500 adjusted for inflation), or allowable itemized deductions directly connected with the unearned income, whichever is greater? *§1(g)(4)(A)*
→ No

Yes (net unearned income) ↓

Does the net unearned income exceed the child's taxable income for the year? *§1(g)(4)(B)*
No →

Yes (up to taxable income) ↓

Kiddie Tax applies. Child's net unearned income is taxed at the greater of the child's regular rate OR the rate at which it would be taxed to the parents if added to their other income. *§1(g)(1)*. It is taxed to the child, not the parents. But see §1(g)(7).

⌐→ + the rate 1(i)(4)

Kiddie Tax does not apply.

Notes

142

Credits Against Taxes
Overview
15.0

Premise
The final step in computing tax liability is to reduce "pre-credits tax liability" by any tax credits allowed. Some credits are *non-refundable* credits (i.e., they can reduce tax liability no lower than $0). Others are *refundable* credits (i.e., they can trigger a refund if the credit exceeds tax liability). This Map points to other maps that provide more detailed treatments of five of the many credits found in the Code.

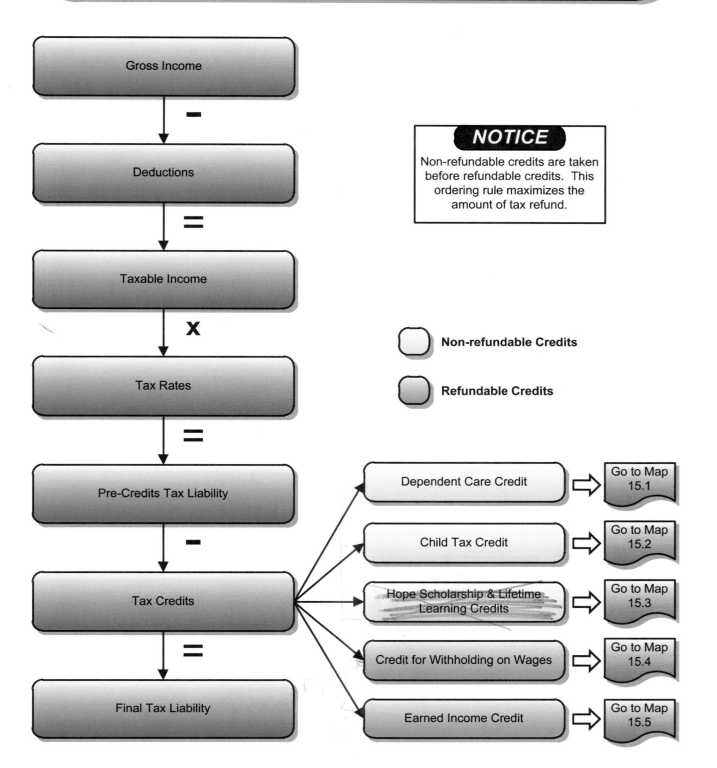

NOTICE

Non-refundable credits are taken before refundable credits. This ordering rule maximizes the amount of tax refund.

⬭ **Non-refundable Credits**

⬭ **Refundable Credits**

Gross Income

−

Deductions

=

Taxable Income

x

Tax Rates

=

Pre-Credits Tax Liability

−

Tax Credits

=

Final Tax Liability

Dependent Care Credit → Go to Map 15.1

Child Tax Credit → Go to Map 15.2

Hope Scholarship & Lifetime Learning Credits → Go to Map 15.3

Credit for Withholding on Wages → Go to Map 15.4

Earned Income Credit → Go to Map 15.5

Notes

Dependent Care Credit
15.1

NOTICE

In the case of divorced parents, the custodial parent is entitled to the credit. *§21(e)(5)*

NOTICE

Expenses for care *outside taxpayer's home* are taken into account only for a qualifying child under the age of 13 or a mentally or physically handicapped dependent or spouse who *regularly spends at least 8 hours each day in taxpayer's household*. *§21(b)(2)*

Employment-Related Expenses
Did taxpayer incur expenses for *household services* or expenses for the *care* of another individual? *§21(b)(2)* — **No**

↓ **Yes**

Qualifying Individual
Was the individual for whom such expenses were incurred:
1. A *qualifying child* of the taxpayer who is under the age of 13; or
2. A *mentally or physically handicapped dependent* or *spouse* of taxpayer who has the same principal place of abode as taxpayer for more than one-half of the year? *§21(b)(1)*. For the definitions of "qualifying child" and "dependent," see Map 10.1. [Note: Relationship with taxpayer cannot be in violation of local law. *§21(e)*.] — **No**

↓ **Yes**

Gainfully Employed
Were the expenses for household services or care incurred to enable taxpayer to be *gainfully employed*? — **No**

↓ **Yes**

No — **Married Taxpayers**
Was taxpayer married at the close of the year?

↓ **Yes**

Did taxpayer and his or her spouse file a joint return for the year? *§21(e)(2)* — **No**

↓ **Yes**

Earned Income Limits
No — Did the expenses for household and dependent care services exceed the lesser of (1) taxpayer's earned income, or (2) the earned income of his or her spouse for the year? *§21(d)(1)(B)*. [The Code imputes earned income to a spouse who is a student or incapable of caring for himself. *§21(d)(2)*.] — **Yes** ⟶ As to excess only

↓

No — Did the expenses for household and dependent care services exceed taxpayer's earned income for the year? *§21(d)(1)(A)* — **Yes** ⟶ As to excess only

Taxpayer is entitled to a dependent care credit equal to:

Employment-related expenses **X** 35%
↓   ↓
• $3,000 cap if 1 qualifying individual
• $6,000 cap if > 1 qualifying individual
• Reduced (but not below 20%) for each $2,000 by which AGI exceeds $15,000. *§21(a)(2)*

Taxpayer is not entitled to the §21 credit.

Notes

Child Tax Credit
15.2

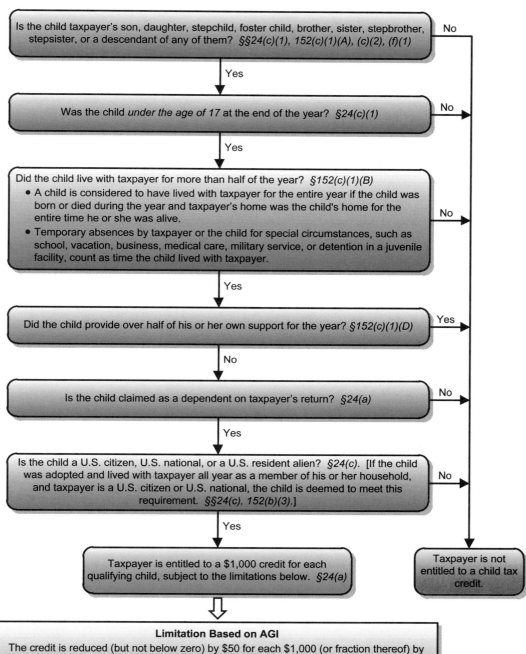

Is the child taxpayer's son, daughter, stepchild, foster child, brother, sister, stepbrother, stepsister, or a descendant of any of them? *§§24(c)(1), 152(c)(1)(A), (c)(2), (f)(1)* — **No** →

↓ **Yes**

Was the child *under the age of 17* at the end of the year? *§24(c)(1)* — **No** →

↓ **Yes**

Did the child live with taxpayer for more than half of the year? *§152(c)(1)(B)*
- A child is considered to have lived with taxpayer for the entire year if the child was born or died during the year and taxpayer's home was the child's home for the entire time he or she was alive.
- Temporary absences by taxpayer or the child for special circumstances, such as school, vacation, business, medical care, military service, or detention in a juvenile facility, count as time the child lived with taxpayer.

— **No** →

↓ **Yes**

Did the child provide over half of his or her own support for the year? *§152(c)(1)(D)* — **Yes** →

↓ **No**

Is the child claimed as a dependent on taxpayer's return? *§24(a)* — **No** →

↓ **Yes**

Is the child a U.S. citizen, U.S. national, or a U.S. resident alien? *§24(c)*. [If the child was adopted and lived with taxpayer all year as a member of his or her household, and taxpayer is a U.S. citizen or U.S. national, the child is deemed to meet this requirement. *§§24(c), 152(b)(3)*.] — **No** →

↓ **Yes**

Taxpayer is entitled to a $1,000 credit for each qualifying child, subject to the limitations below. *§24(a)*

Taxpayer is not entitled to a child tax credit.

Limitation Based on AGI

The credit is reduced (but not below zero) by $50 for each $1,000 (or fraction thereof) by which taxpayer's AGI exceeds the following *threshold amount*:
- Married filing jointly à $110,000.
- Single, head of household à $75,000.
- Married filing separately à $55,000. *§24(b)(2)*

Limitation Based on Tax Liability

In most cases, the credit is *non-refundable* and cannot bring tax liability below $0. *§24(b)(3)*. [NOTE: In certain cases, the remaining unused credit is not lost, but is *refundable*. The additional child tax credit is the lesser of the unused credit or 15% of taxpayer's earned income in excess of $3,000 (if taxpayer has one or more qualifying children). *§24(d)(1)(B)(i)*. A taxpayer with three or more children may receive a more generous refund. *§24(d)(1)(B)(ii)*.]

147

Notes

Hope Scholarship and
Lifetime Learning Credits
15.3

149

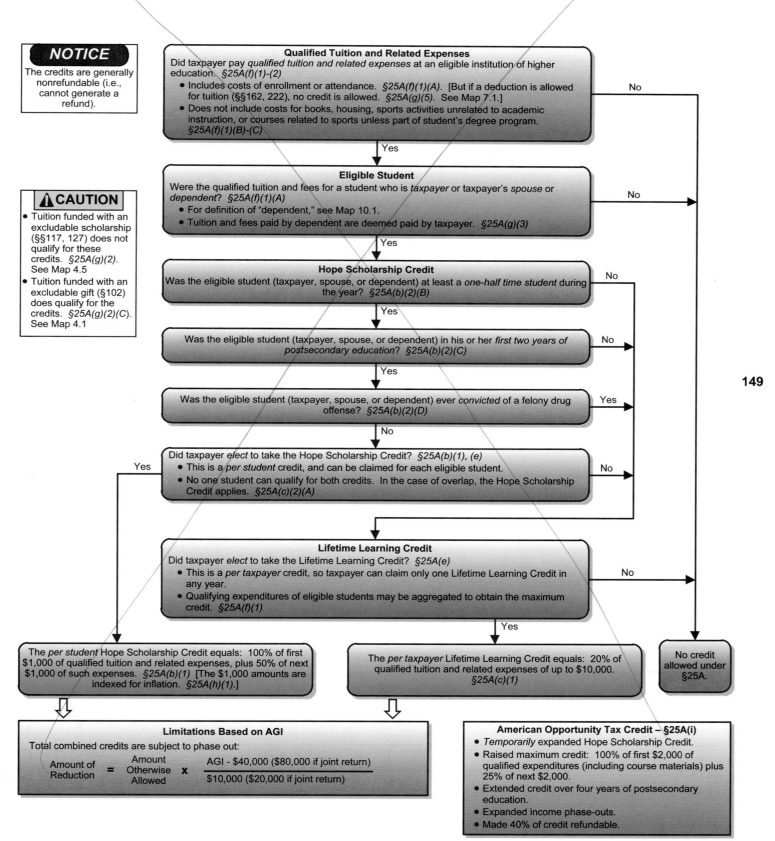

NOTICE

The credits are generally nonrefundable (i.e., cannot generate a refund).

⚠ CAUTION

- Tuition funded with an excludable scholarship (§§117, 127) does not qualify for these credits. *§25A(g)(2)*. See Map 4.5
- Tuition funded with an excludable gift (§102) does qualify for the credits. *§25A(g)(2)(C)*. See Map 4.1

Qualified Tuition and Related Expenses
Did taxpayer pay *qualified tuition and related expenses* at an eligible institution of higher education. *§25A(f)(1)-(2)*
- Includes costs of enrollment or attendance. *§25A(f)(1)(A)*. [But if a deduction is allowed for tuition (§§162, 222), no credit is allowed. *§25A(g)(5)*. See Map 7.1.]
- Does not include costs for books, housing, sports activities unrelated to academic instruction, or courses related to sports unless part of student's degree program. *§25A(f)(1)(B)-(C)*

→ No

Yes ↓

Eligible Student
Were the qualified tuition and fees for a student who is *taxpayer* or taxpayer's *spouse* or *dependent*? *§25A(f)(1)(A)*
- For definition of "dependent," see Map 10.1.
- Tuition and fees paid by dependent are deemed paid by taxpayer. *§25A(g)(3)*

→ No

Yes ↓

Hope Scholarship Credit
Was the eligible student (taxpayer, spouse, or dependent) at least a *one-half time student* during the year? *§25A(b)(2)(B)*

→ No

Yes ↓

Was the eligible student (taxpayer, spouse, or dependent) in his or her *first two years of postsecondary education*? *§25A(b)(2)(C)*

→ No

Yes ↓

Was the eligible student (taxpayer, spouse, or dependent) ever *convicted* of a felony drug offense? *§25A(b)(2)(D)*

→ Yes

No ↓

Did taxpayer *elect* to take the Hope Scholarship Credit? *§25A(b)(1), (e)*
- This is a *per student* credit, and can be claimed for each eligible student.
- No one student can qualify for both credits. In the case of overlap, the Hope Scholarship Credit applies. *§25A(c)(2)(A)*

Yes ←   → No

Lifetime Learning Credit
Did taxpayer *elect* to take the Lifetime Learning Credit? *§25A(e)*
- This is a *per taxpayer* credit, so taxpayer can claim only one Lifetime Learning Credit in any year.
- Qualifying expenditures of eligible students may be aggregated to obtain the maximum credit. *§25A(f)(1)*

→ No

Yes ↓

The *per student* Hope Scholarship Credit equals: 100% of first $1,000 of qualified tuition and related expenses, plus 50% of next $1,000 of such expenses. *§25A(b)(1)* [The $1,000 amounts are indexed for inflation. *§25A(h)(1)*.]

The *per taxpayer* Lifetime Learning Credit equals: 20% of qualified tuition and related expenses of up to $10,000. *§25A(c)(1)*

No credit allowed under §25A.

Limitations Based on AGI
Total combined credits are subject to phase out:

$$\text{Amount of Reduction} = \text{Amount Otherwise Allowed} \times \frac{\text{AGI} - \$40,000\ (\$80,000\ \text{if joint return})}{\$10,000\ (\$20,000\ \text{if joint return})}$$

American Opportunity Tax Credit – §25A(i)
- *Temporarily* expanded Hope Scholarship Credit.
- Raised maximum credit: 100% of first $2,000 of qualified expenditures (including course materials) plus 25% of next $2,000.
- Extended credit over four years of postsecondary education.
- Expanded income phase-outs.
- Made 40% of credit refundable.

Notes

150

Credit for Withholding on Wages
15.4

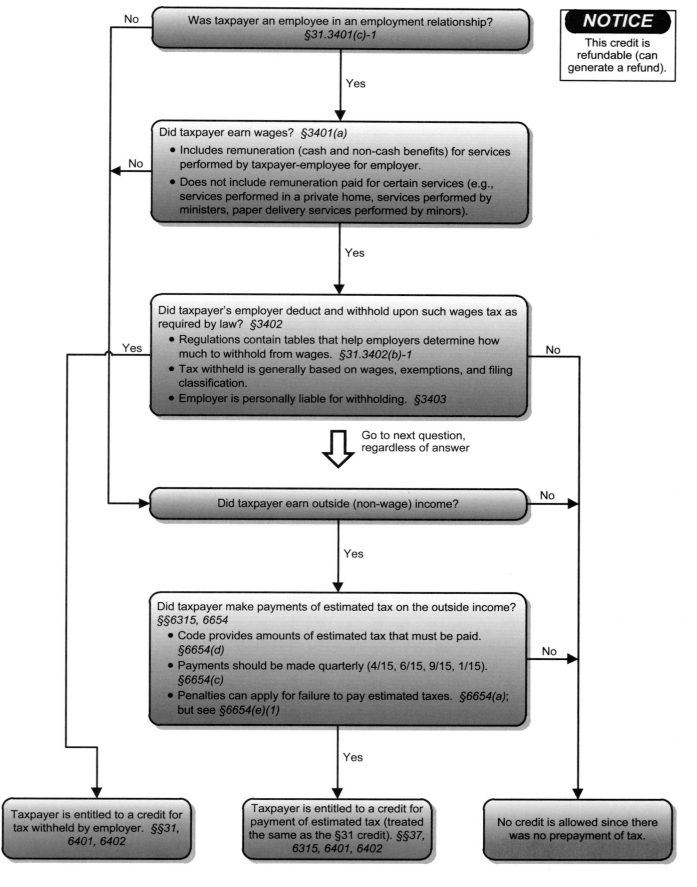

Was taxpayer an employee in an employment relationship? *§31.3401(c)-1*

No → / Yes ↓

NOTICE
This credit is refundable (can generate a refund).

Did taxpayer earn wages? *§3401(a)*
- Includes remuneration (cash and non-cash benefits) for services performed by taxpayer-employee for employer.
- Does not include remuneration paid for certain services (e.g., services performed in a private home, services performed by ministers, paper delivery services performed by minors).

No ← / Yes ↓

Did taxpayer's employer deduct and withhold upon such wages tax as required by law? *§3402*
- Regulations contain tables that help employers determine how much to withhold from wages. *§31.3402(b)-1*
- Tax withheld is generally based on wages, exemptions, and filing classification.
- Employer is personally liable for withholding. *§3403*

Yes / No

Go to next question, regardless of answer

Did taxpayer earn outside (non-wage) income?

No →

Yes ↓

Did taxpayer make payments of estimated tax on the outside income? *§§6315, 6654*
- Code provides amounts of estimated tax that must be paid. *§6654(d)*
- Payments should be made quarterly (4/15, 6/15, 9/15, 1/15). *§6654(c)*
- Penalties can apply for failure to pay estimated taxes. *§6654(a)*; but see *§6654(e)(1)*

No →

Yes ↓

Taxpayer is entitled to a credit for tax withheld by employer. *§§31, 6401, 6402*

Taxpayer is entitled to a credit for payment of estimated tax (treated the same as the §31 credit). *§§37, 6315, 6401, 6402*

No credit is allowed since there was no prepayment of tax.

151

Notes

Earned Income Credit
15.5

NOTICE
This credit is a refundable credit (can generate a refund).

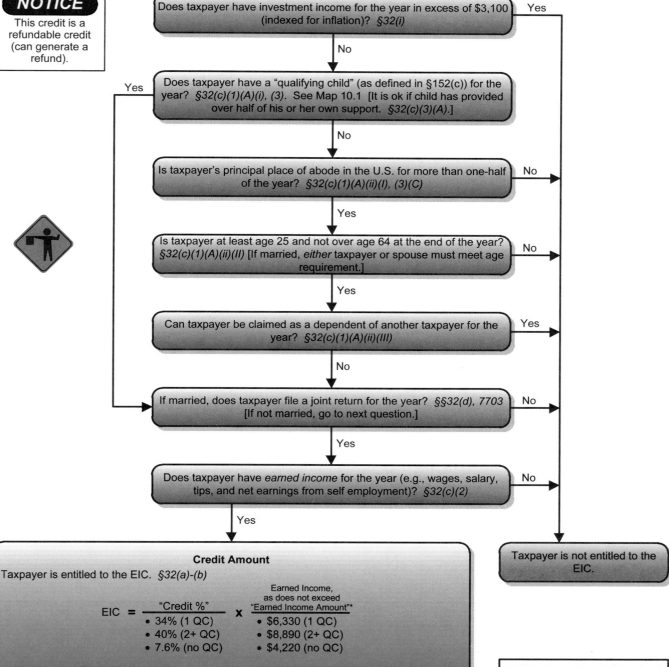

Does taxpayer have investment income for the year in excess of $3,100 (indexed for inflation)? *§32(i)* — **Yes** →

No ↓

Does taxpayer have a "qualifying child" (as defined in §152(c)) for the year? *§32(c)(1)(A)(i), (3)*. See Map 10.1 [It is ok if child has provided over half of his or her own support. *§32(c)(3)(A)*.] — **Yes** →

No ↓

Is taxpayer's principal place of abode in the U.S. for more than one-half of the year? *§32(c)(1)(A)(ii)(I), (3)(C)* — **No** →

Yes ↓

Is taxpayer at least age 25 and not over age 64 at the end of the year? *§32(c)(1)(A)(ii)(II)* [If married, *either* taxpayer or spouse must meet age requirement.] — **No** →

Yes ↓

Can taxpayer be claimed as a dependent of another taxpayer for the year? *§32(c)(1)(A)(ii)(III)* — **Yes** →

No ↓

If married, does taxpayer file a joint return for the year? *§§32(d), 7703* [If not married, go to next question.] — **No** →

Yes ↓

Does taxpayer have *earned income* for the year (e.g., wages, salary, tips, and net earnings from self employment)? *§32(c)(2)* — **No** →

Yes ↓

Credit Amount
Taxpayer is entitled to the EIC. *§32(a)-(b)*

$$\text{EIC} = \text{"Credit \%"} \times \text{Earned Income, as does not exceed "Earned Income Amount"*}$$

"Credit %"
- 34% (1 QC)
- 40% (2+ QC)
- 7.6% (no QC)

Earned Income, as does not exceed "Earned Income Amount"*
- $6,330 (1 QC)
- $8,890 (2+ QC)
- $4,220 (no QC)

*Amount adjusted for inflation.

⇩

Phase-Outs
The credit is phased-out by a % of earned income in excess of a "phase-out" amount:

$$\text{Max EIC} = \left[\begin{array}{c} \text{Credit \%} \\ \times \\ \text{Earned Income Amount} \end{array} \right] - \left[\text{"Phased Out \%"} \times \left(\text{Greater of: Earned Income or AGI} - \text{"Phased Amount"*} \right) \right]$$

"Phased Out %"
- 15.98% (1 QC)
- 21.06% (2+ QC)
- 7.65% (no QC)

"Phased Amount"*
- $11,610 (1 QC)
- $11,610 (2+ QC)
- $5,280 (no QC)

*Amounts adjusted for inflation.

Taxpayer is not entitled to the EIC.

Temporary Enhancements
In the past, Congress has temporarily enhanced the credit.

- The earned income credit % increased from 40% to 45% for taxpayers with 3 or more qualifying children. *§32(b)(3)(A)*

- The phase-out amounts increased by $5,000 for joint filers. *§32(b)(3)(B)*

Notes

154

TABLE OF CASES

TABLE OF ABBREVIATIONS

AB: adjusted basis

AGI: adjusted gross income

AR: amount realized

CB: contribution base

DOI: discharge of indebtedness

DPF: disfavored private foundation

EIC: earned income credit

FMV: fair market value

H/P: holding period

LTCG: long term capital gain

LTCL: long term capital loss

NCG: net capital gain

NLTCG: net long term capital gain

NLTCL: net long term capital loss

NSTCG: net short term capital gain

NSTCL: net short term capital loss

PG: part gift

PPOB: principal place of business

PS: part sale

QC: qualifying child

STCG: short term capital gain

STCL: short term capital loss

This Page Left Intentionally Blank

INDEX

160